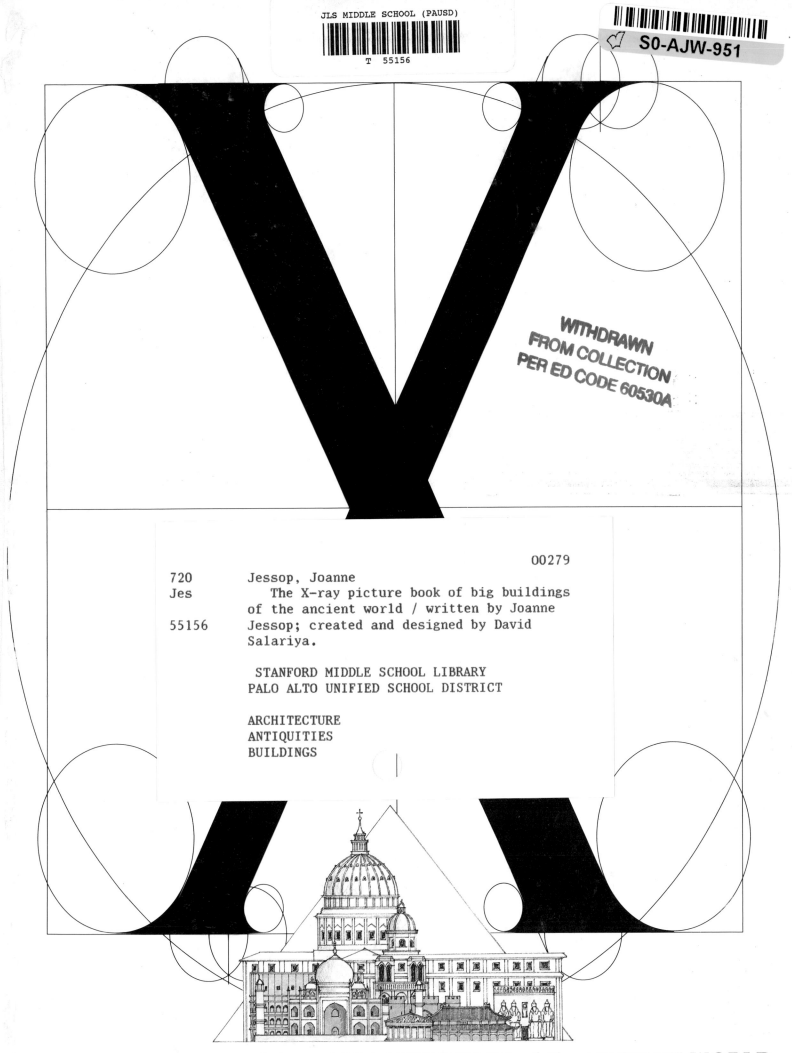

THE X-RAY PICTURE BOOK *of* BIG BUILDINGS *of the* ANCIENT WORLD

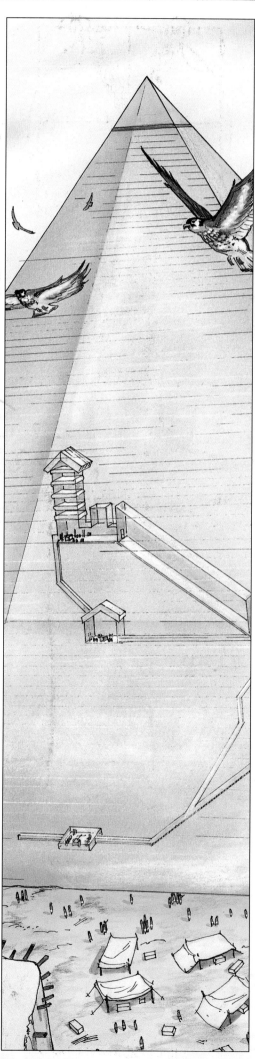

Author:

Joanne Jessop holds an undergraduate degree from the University of Waterloo in Ontario, Canada, and a master's degree from the University of British Columbia in Canada. She has many years' experience as a writer and editor of children's reference books and specializes in historical and biographical books for children.

Creator:

David Salariya was born in Dundee, Scotland, where he studied illustration and printmaking, concentrating on book design in his post-graduate year. He has illustrated a wide range of books on botanical, historical and mythical subjects. He has designed and created the *Timelines*, *New View* and *X-ray Picture Book* series for Watts. He lives in Brighton with his wife, the illustrator Shirley Willis.

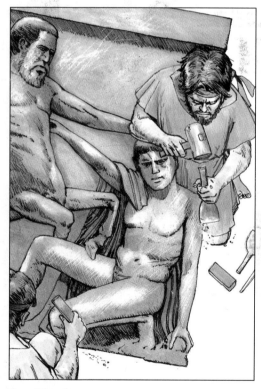

Franklin Watts
95 Madison Avenue
New York, NY 10016

David Salariya	*Series Editor*
Ruth Taylor	*Senior Editor*
Vicki Power	*Book Editor*
David Robson	*Consultant*

Artists:

Mark Bergin

Dean Entwistle

Nick Hewetson

Graham Humphreys

Kevin Maddison

Clyde Pearson

Gerald Wood

Artists

Mark Bergin 6-7, 40-41; **Dean Entwistle** 22-23, 42-43; **Nick Hewetson** 10-11, 24-25, 34-35, 36-37, 38-39; **Graham Humphreys** 26-27; **Kevin Maddison** 14-15, 18-19; **Clyde Pearson** 8-9, 12-13; **Gerald Wood** 16-17, 20-21, 28-29, 30-31, 32-33.

© The Salariya Book Co Ltd 1993

Library of Congress Cataloging-in-Publication Data

Jessop, Joanne.
    Big buildings of the ancient world / written by Joanne Jessop; created and designed by David Salariya.
        p.   cm. (The X-ray picture book)
    Includes index.
        ISBN 0-531-14286-8 (lib.bdg.) – ISBN 0-531-15709-1 (pbk.)
        1. Monuments – History – Juvenile literature.
    [1. Buildings. 2. Antiquities.] I. Salariya, David.
    II. Title. III. Title: Big buildings of the ancient world.
NA200.J47 1994
720–dc20
                                                    93-36704
                                                    CIP AC

The X RAY PICTURE BOOK of BIG BUILDINGS of the ANCIENT WORLD

Written by
JOANNE JESSOP

Created and designed by
DAVID SALARIYA

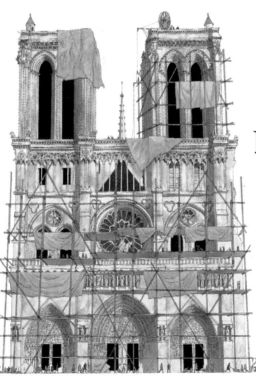

FRANKLIN WATTS

NEW YORK · CHICAGO · LONDON · TORONTO · SYDNEY

CONTENTS

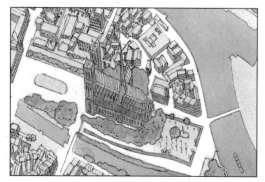

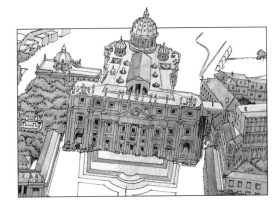

In this book, the term "ancient buildings" refers to buildings that were built before the seventeenth century. Big buildings built after that are featured in *The X-ray Picture Book of Big Buildings of the Modern World*.

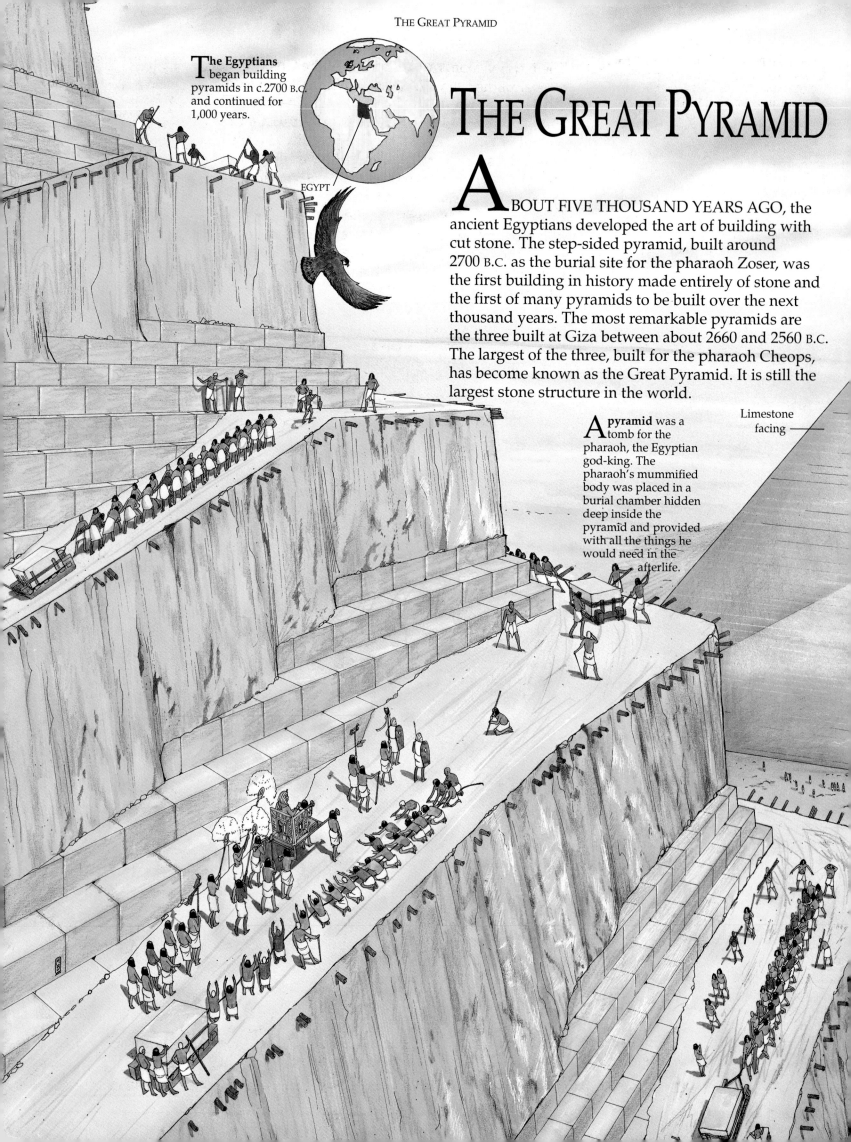

THE GREAT PYRAMID

The Egyptians began building pyramids in c.2700 B.C. and continued for 1,000 years.

EGYPT

ABOUT FIVE THOUSAND YEARS AGO, the ancient Egyptians developed the art of building with cut stone. The step-sided pyramid, built around 2700 B.C. as the burial site for the pharaoh Zoser, was the first building in history made entirely of stone and the first of many pyramids to be built over the next thousand years. The most remarkable pyramids are the three built at Giza between about 2660 and 2560 B.C. The largest of the three, built for the pharaoh Cheops, has become known as the Great Pyramid. It is still the largest stone structure in the world.

A pyramid was a tomb for the pharaoh, the Egyptian god-king. The pharaoh's mummified body was placed in a burial chamber hidden deep inside the pyramid and provided with all the things he would need in the afterlife.

Limestone facing

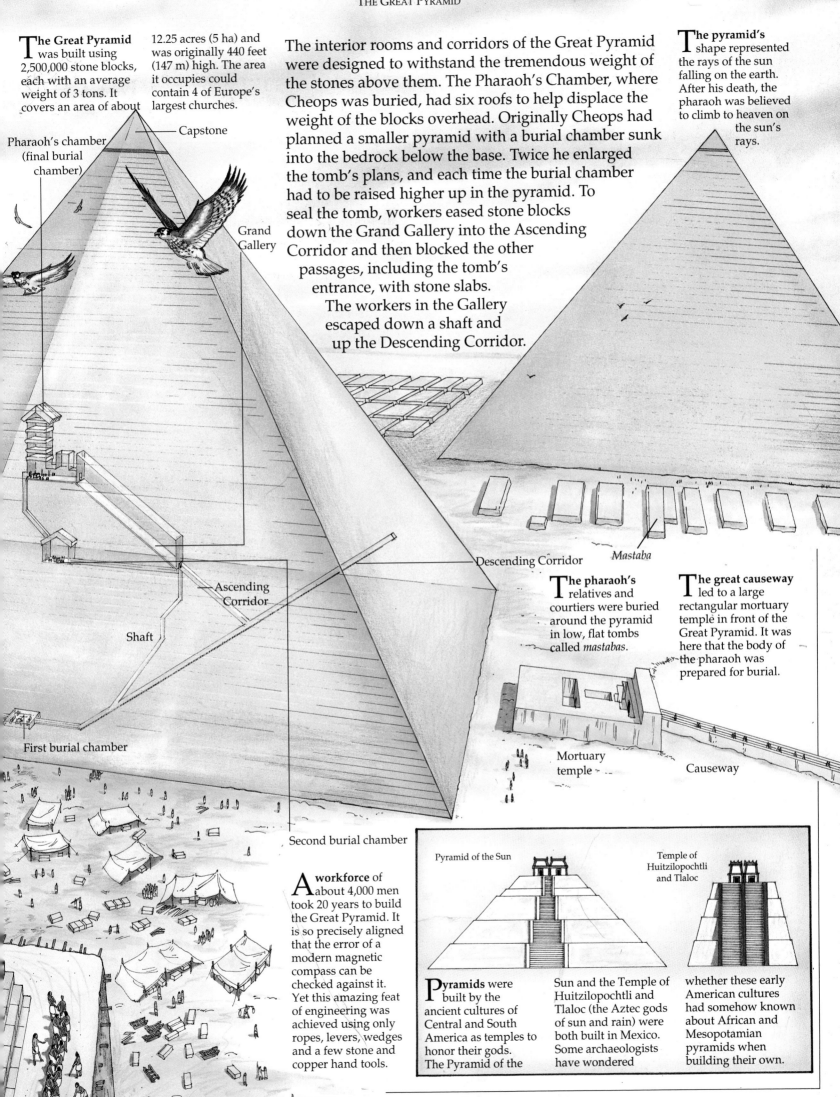

The Great Pyramid was built using 2,500,000 stone blocks, each with an average weight of 3 tons. It covers an area of about 12.25 acres (5 ha) and was originally 440 feet (147 m) high. The area it occupies could contain 4 of Europe's largest churches.

Capstone

Pharaoh's chamber (final burial chamber)

Grand Gallery

The interior rooms and corridors of the Great Pyramid were designed to withstand the tremendous weight of the stones above them. The Pharaoh's Chamber, where Cheops was buried, had six roofs to help displace the weight of the blocks overhead. Originally Cheops had planned a smaller pyramid with a burial chamber sunk into the bedrock below the base. Twice he enlarged the tomb's plans, and each time the burial chamber had to be raised higher up in the pyramid. To seal the tomb, workers eased stone blocks down the Grand Gallery into the Ascending Corridor and then blocked the other passages, including the tomb's entrance, with stone slabs. The workers in the Gallery escaped down a shaft and up the Descending Corridor.

The pyramid's shape represented the rays of the sun falling on the earth. After his death, the pharaoh was believed to climb to heaven on the sun's rays.

Ascending Corridor

Shaft

First burial chamber

Descending Corridor

Mastaba

The pharaoh's relatives and courtiers were buried around the pyramid in low, flat tombs called mastabas.

The great causeway led to a large rectangular mortuary temple in front of the Great Pyramid. It was here that the body of the pharaoh was prepared for burial.

Mortuary temple

Causeway

Second burial chamber

A workforce of about 4,000 men took 20 years to build the Great Pyramid. It is so precisely aligned that the error of a modern magnetic compass can be checked against it. Yet this amazing feat of engineering was achieved using only ropes, levers, wedges and a few stone and copper hand tools.

Pyramid of the Sun

Temple of Huitzilopochtli and Tlaloc

Pyramids were built by the ancient cultures of Central and South America as temples to honor their gods. The Pyramid of the Sun and the Temple of Huitzilopochtli and Tlaloc (the Aztec gods of sun and rain) were both built in Mexico. Some archaeologists have wondered whether these early American cultures had somehow known about African and Mesopotamian pyramids when building their own.

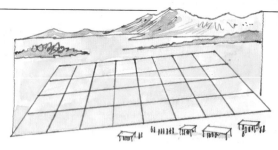

A pyramid took many years to complete, so the pharaoh would order work to begin on his pyramid long before he expected to die. He would send his officials to find a suitable site and order his architect to begin making designs.

A circular wall was built as an artificial horizon from which a priest observed the stars to find true north.

When the position of the pyramid had been chosen, the pharaoh performed a ritual ceremony at the site.

The pyramid had to be built on level ground. After the base of the pyramid was marked out, a crisscross of channels was cut across the site and filled with water. Rocks protruding above the waterline were cut away. The channels were later filled in with rubble.

The pyramids were built west of the Nile in the land of the dead. The remains of more than 80 have been found.

BUILDING THE
Great Pyramid

Wooden wedges were put into grooves cut in the quarry walls. The wedges were soaked with water, causing the wood to expand and split off the block of stone.

Masons' and quarrymen's tools (below): Plumblines (A, F); Bow drill (B); Set square (C); Mallet (D); Chisel (E).

THE STONES FOR THE PYRAMIDS were cut in quarries, loaded onto barges and towed by rowing boats along the Nile. The blocks were hauled from the river to the building site along a specially built causeway. The pyramid was built around a central core. Gaps were left for corridors, airshafts and burial chambers. These interior structures had to be designed to carry the massive weight of the stones above them. Local limestone was used to build the core of the pyramid, but the best quality limestone was shipped from quarries across the Nile to make the pyramid's outer casing. These casing blocks were placed with such extreme accuracy that a razor blade can hardly be inserted between them.

The thousands of men required to do the dangerous work of quarrying and hauling the huge stone blocks were not slaves. Some were convicts or prisoners of war, but most were ordinary farmers. A certain number were summoned each year by the pharaoh's officials to join the pyramid workforce. They worked willingly to build a pyramid that would protect the pharaoh's body for all eternity. With a pharaoh who lived forever in the land of the gods, Egypt would enjoy every blessing a god could give.

The ancient Egyptians built the pyramids without the use of the wheel or draft animals. Blocks of stone were levered onto sledges, which were hauled from the quarry over a path of logs to barges on the Nile.

A worker's daily rations (above): bread, beer and scallions.

Farmers worked the land and planted their crops after the floodwaters of the Nile had receded. Without the annual floods, the land would have become a desert.

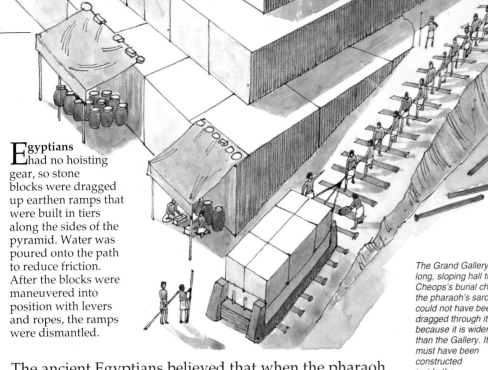

Egyptians had no hoisting gear, so stone blocks were dragged up earthen ramps that were built in tiers along the sides of the pyramid. Water was poured onto the path to reduce friction. After the blocks were maneuvered into position with levers and ropes, the ramps were dismantled.

The Grand Gallery was a long, sloping hall that led to Cheops's burial chamber. But the pharaoh's sarcophagus could not have been dragged through it because it is wider than the Gallery. It must have been constructed inside the burial chamber.

The capstone ceremony (above). The pharaoh was carried to the top of the pyramid, where the capstone was waiting on wooden blocks. During the ceremony the blocks were removed and the capstone dropped into place.

The ancient Egyptians believed that when the pharaoh died, his spirit would go on living in the land of the dead. But, without the body to rest in, the pharaoh's soul would perish. In order to stop the body from decaying, it had to be carefully preserved by making it into what we now call a mummy. The mummified body of the pharaoh was protected within the pyramid, where it was provided with articles such as food, clothes, weapons, furniture and jewelry that the soul would need in the afterlife.

Grand Gallery

When a pharaoh died his mummified body was taken by special boat to his pyramid in the land of the dead on the west side of the Nile (below). This journey followed the same path as that of the sun-god who traveled every day across the sky and disappeared in the west to begin his journey through the underworld.

Mummification followed a strict ritual. The man who cut open the pharaoh's abdomen to remove the internal organs was called the ripper. He was then stoned and driven away.

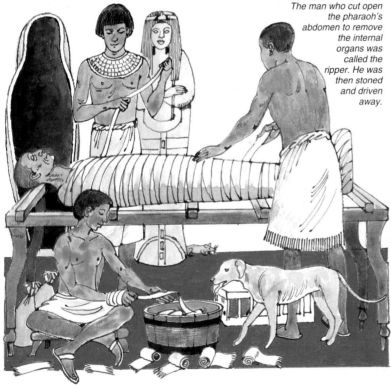

The ceremony of the opening of the mouth (below) was performed on the day of the funeral. Priests, including the pharaoh's son, touched parts of the mummy with special ritual instruments. This ceremony gave back to the mummy all its bodily senses so that the pharaoh would be able to speak, see, hear, breathe and move in the afterlife.

Mummies were placed in coffins made from hollowed logs.

When a pharaoh died his body was mummified. Internal organs, which would make the body rot, were removed and stored in jars. The brain was removed through the nose. The corpse was packed in natron (a type of salt) for 40 days to dry out. It was then bound tightly in resin-soaked linen. If any part of the body rotted, it was replaced with linen wads. The mummy was then placed in a coffin.

The temple at Abu Simbel was the first Egyptian temple to be built into the side of a cliff. Nevertheless, it followed the same basic layout as temples built in the open.

Artists decorated the temple walls with hieroglyphs and reliefs that told of Rameses' life and his achievements. Many of the scenes glorified Rameses' victories in battle. Clerks dressed in white linen garments checked the artists' work against the official plans and sent progress reports down the Nile to the pharaoh.

The seated figures of Rameses are over 65 feet (20 m) high and weigh over 1,000 tons. The small figures standing at Rameses' feet are some members of the royal family.

For the ancient Egyptians, a huge statue, or colossus, was the living embodiment of the person or god it represented.

ABU SIMBEL

In 1250 B.C., WHEN THE GREAT PYRAMID at Giza had already stood for over a thousand years in the desert sands, Rameses II ordered a magnificent temple to be built at Abu Simbel to commemorate the thirtieth year of his reign.

In the inner sanctum of the temple, four seated figures were hewn out of the rock. They represented Rameses seated with Re-Harakhti, the sun god, on his left, and with Amun, the god of Thebes, and Ptah, the god of Memphis, on his right. Draftsmen first traced sketches of the statues on smoothed walls. Sculptors chiseled the statues from the rock. Painters then applied bright colors to the statues.

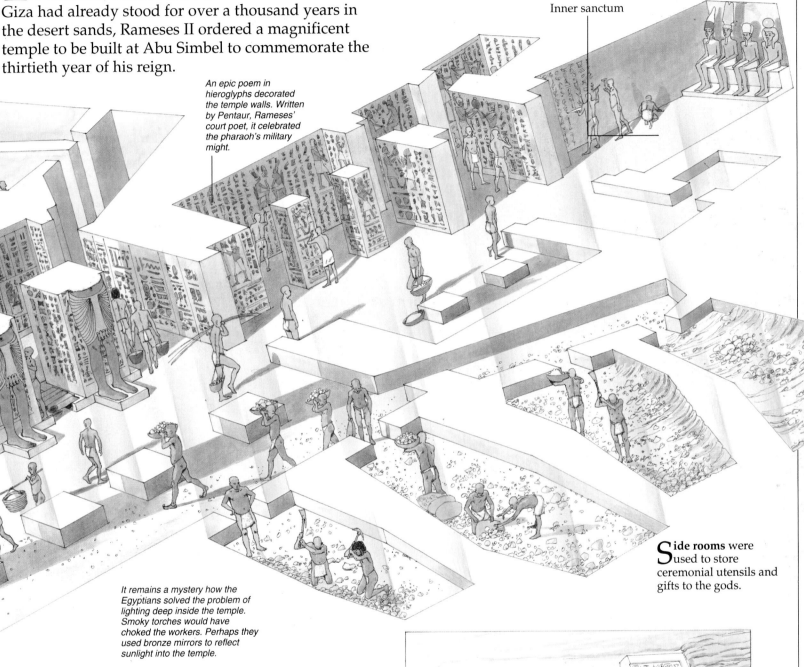

An epic poem in hieroglyphs decorated the temple walls. Written by Pentaur, Rameses' court poet, it celebrated the pharaoh's military might.

Inner sanctum

It remains a mystery how the Egyptians solved the problem of lighting deep inside the temple. Smoky torches would have choked the workers. Perhaps they used bronze mirrors to reflect sunlight into the temple.

Side rooms were used to store ceremonial utensils and gifts to the gods.

The entire temple was carved into sandstone cliffs rising above the banks of the Nile. Four giant seated figures of Rameses guard the temple entrance; inside the temple, three adjoining halls extend 170 feet (56 m) into the cliffs. The temple was designed so that on October 21, the anniversary of Rameses' coronation as pharaoh of Egypt, and again on February 21, Rameses' birthday, the rays of the rising sun would penetrate the whole length of the temple and light up the statues of Rameses and the god Amun carved into the back wall of the innermost chamber.

The small temple at Abu Simbel honors Rameses' favorite queen, Nefertari, and the goddess of love, Hathor. The temple is decorated with many images of Nefertari.

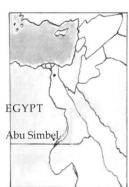

During Rameses' reign, Egyptian civilization was at its peak. Rameses' kingdom spread from present-day Syria to the Sudan. Rameses II, called "the Great," ruled Egypt for 67 years. He won wars that added territory and wealth to his kingdom.

The palace architects and engineers (left) prepared plans for a temple in honor of Rameses II and a smaller one dedicated to his wife, Nefertari.

Boats sailed up the Nile, carrying men and equipment to start work on the royal temple. Everything had to be transported by boat to this isolated spot at the edge of civilization.

BUILDING
Abu Simbel

THE TEMPLES OF ANCIENT EGYPT were houses for the gods, who were represented as statues. Gods were believed to have the same needs as humans, and it was the duty of the temple priests to serve these needs. Every morning the priests would wash, dress and offer food to the small image of the temple god.

Because the pharaoh was considered to be both king and god, he would often be honored among the temple gods. But at Abu Simbel, Rameses II was the major object of worship. Although the temple was dedicated to the sun god Re-Harakhti, images of Rameses are seen everywhere. The temple was built to glorify his power and greatness and stood alone at the edge of his kingdom to warn off any enemies who might dare to invade. No crowds of worshipers gathered here; only temple priests served at this outpost. In fact, there is no evidence that Rameses himself ever visited Abu Simbel.

Engineers lined up the axis of the temple so that twice a year the rays of the rising sun shone directly onto the back wall of the innermost chamber. A red line was drawn onto the cliff face to show the path of the sun's rays.

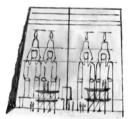

Stonecutters chiseled the cliff face into a smooth surface, on which a grid was drawn to help the draftsmen proportion the collossi.

Masons chipped away the background so that blocks emerged from the cliff face that represented feet, legs, arms and a head.

Master sculptors set to work with mallets and bronze chisels, carving the shapes into giant figures of Rameses.

When the sculptors had finished their work, painters applied bright colors, following strict rules of temple decoration.

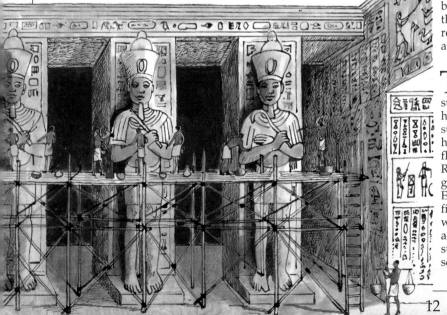

The pillars that served as ceiling supports for the great hall were carved into statues of Rameses holding the crook and flail, symbols of Rameses and Osiris, god of the Nile. Like all Egyptian temple figures, these colossi were painted according to a standardized color scheme.

Stonecutters, using tools of bronze and hardwood, hollowed the temple out of the sandstone cliff, leaving pillars in place as ceiling supports. In the great hall, sculptors carved the eight supporting pillars into 30-foot (10 m)-tall statues of Rameses. In the adjoining hall, the pillars were carved into four smooth sides and decorated with paintings.

Twice a year, in late February and late October, the rays of the rising sun reach 100 feet (32 m) into the back of the temple and light up the statues of Rameses and the god Amun.

The cartouche of Rameses II was an oval emblem of hieroglyphs (pictorial writing) that gave the pharaoh's birth name and coronation name.

A smaller temple to Nefertari was built at the same time. The entrance to the temple is flanked by two statues of Nefertari and four of Rameses himself.

The upper portion of the second colossus on the south side fell soon after the temple was completed. It has never been repaired or replaced.

According to the inscription on its façade, the small temple at Abu Simbel was built as "a mansion for the great royal wife Nefertari." This temple was a monument to Rameses' great love for his favorite queen. Inside, the temple walls were decorated with images of Nefertari, usually beside her husband. The names of Nefertari and Rameses appear on every pillar.

In the 1960s, the temples at Abu Simbel were under threat from water rising behind the Aswan Dam. The United Nations launched a worldwide appeal to save these historic monuments from flooding. The project began in 1964 under the direction of engineers from five countries and took four years to complete. The temples were cut into 1,050 sections, some weighing over 30 tons, and reassembled on higher ground beneath artificial hills that had been specially designed to resemble the original setting. The temples now stand 200 feet (60 m) higher and 700 feet (210 m) inland from the original shoreline. It was an engineering feat that matched that of the ancient Egyptians.

The new position of the temples, directly above the old sites (below).

THE PARTHENON

Greece

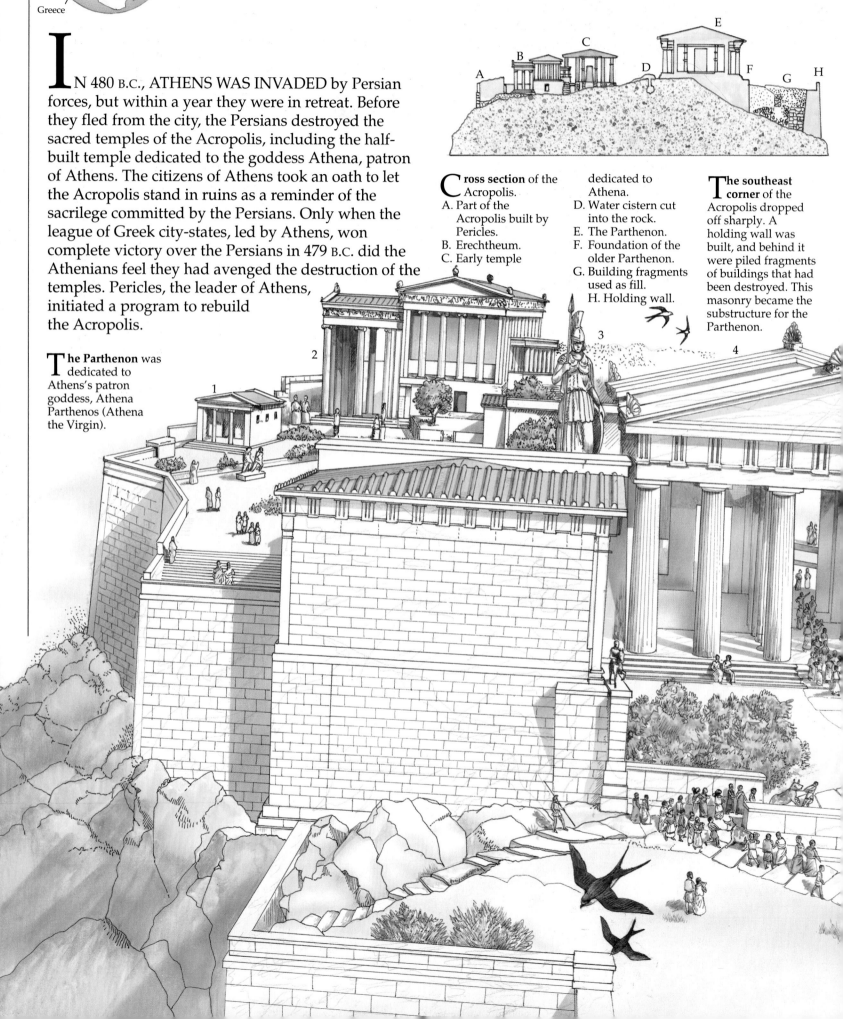

IN 480 B.C., ATHENS WAS INVADED by Persian forces, but within a year they were in retreat. Before they fled from the city, the Persians destroyed the sacred temples of the Acropolis, including the half-built temple dedicated to the goddess Athena, patron of Athens. The citizens of Athens took an oath to let the Acropolis stand in ruins as a reminder of the sacrilege committed by the Persians. Only when the league of Greek city-states, led by Athens, won complete victory over the Persians in 479 B.C. did the Athenians feel they had avenged the destruction of the temples. Pericles, the leader of Athens, initiated a program to rebuild the Acropolis.

The Parthenon was dedicated to Athens's patron goddess, Athena Parthenos (Athena the Virgin).

Cross section of the Acropolis.
A. Part of the Acropolis built by Pericles.
B. Erechtheum.
C. Early temple dedicated to Athena.
D. Water cistern cut into the rock.
E. The Parthenon.
F. Foundation of the older Parthenon.
G. Building fragments used as fill.
H. Holding wall.

The southeast corner of the Acropolis dropped off sharply. A holding wall was built, and behind it were piled fragments of buildings that had been destroyed. This masonry became the substructure for the Parthenon.

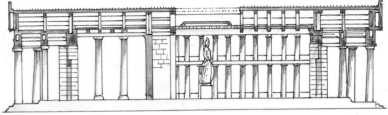

Pericles' most ambitious undertaking was the reconstruction, on a much grander scale, of the temple of Athena Parthenos. The Parthenon was a simple structure – a series of vertical pillars and horizontal lintels. The number and position of the columns followed the precise rules of proportion that applied to all Greek temples. But in the building of the Parthenon, these design criteria were refined and adjusted to create such a sense of balance and harmony that it still ranks as one of the most elegant structures ever built.

The Parthenon was surrounded by columns. Inside the columns, a walkway led around the whole building. The inner chamber was divided into two parts that opened to the outside. The longer eastern chamber, which housed the statue of Athena, had two rows and two tiers of columns. The western chamber had four tall columns and housed the temple treasures. The outer porches were used as state treasuries.

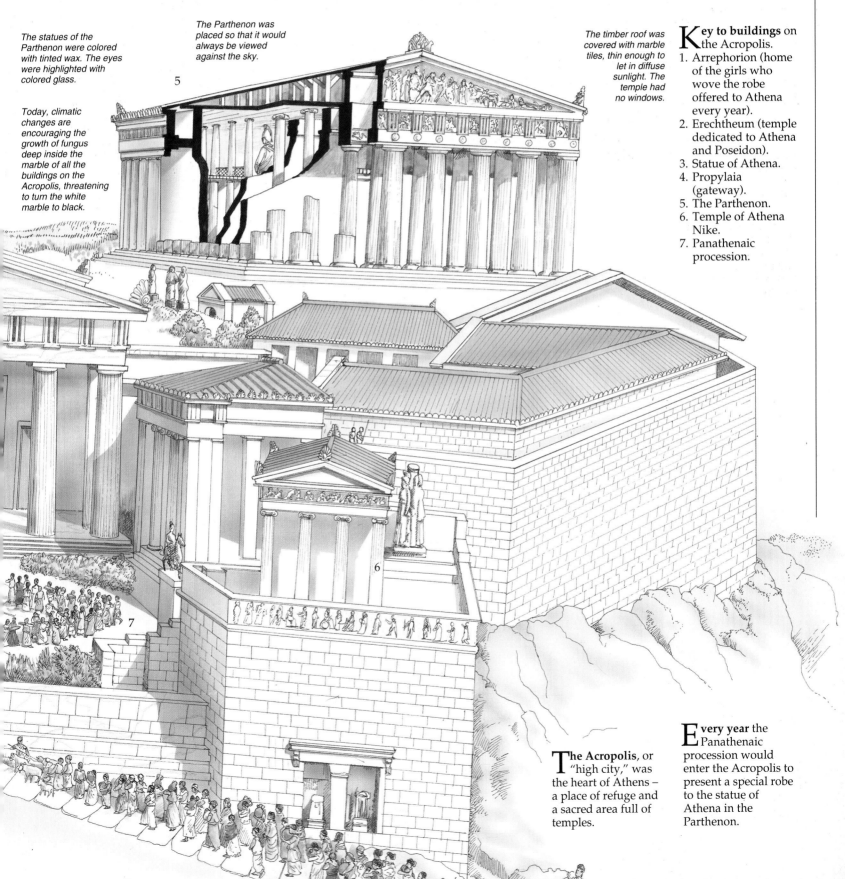

The statues of the Parthenon were colored with tinted wax. The eyes were highlighted with colored glass.

Today, climatic changes are encouraging the growth of fungus deep inside the marble of all the buildings on the Acropolis, threatening to turn the white marble to black.

The Parthenon was placed so that it would always be viewed against the sky.

The timber roof was covered with marble tiles, thin enough to let in diffuse sunlight. The temple had no windows.

Key to buildings on the Acropolis.
1. Arrephorion (home of the girls who wove the robe offered to Athena every year).
2. Erechtheum (temple dedicated to Athena and Poseidon).
3. Statue of Athena.
4. Propylaia (gateway).
5. The Parthenon.
6. Temple of Athena Nike.
7. Panathenaic procession.

The Acropolis, or "high city," was the heart of Athens – a place of refuge and a sacred area full of temples.

Every year the Panathenaic procession would enter the Acropolis to present a special robe to the statue of Athena in the Parthenon.

In 490 B.C., after many years of war, the Persians were defeated by the Athenians in a sea battle. That same year, Persian forces returned to seek revenge.

They invaded Athens and destroyed the sacred temples. In 479 B.C., when the Persians were driven out, the Athenians returned to find the Acropolis in ruins.

In 449 B.C., the Persian wars were finally ended. Pericles, the leader of Athens, proposed that the Acropolis be rebuilt to commemorate the Greek victory.

BUILDING THE
Parthenon

THE ARCHITECTS OF THE PARTHENON made subtle adjustments to create an impression of symmetry. Because a column with perfectly straight sides would appear thinner in the middle, the columns of the Parthenon were made to bulge very slightly. The corner columns were slightly thicker than the rest; otherwise they would look thinner against the open sky. The base of the temple was raised at the center to stop it from looking as if it were sagging. The columns lean inward slightly to draw the eye upward. Even the flutings on each column were tapered as they rose. In fact, there are few straight lines in the whole temple.

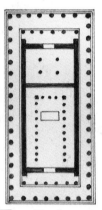

The sides have double the number of columns at the ends, plus one.

Marble was quarried from Mount Pentelicus, and transported the 10 miles (16 km) to Athens on carts pulled by oxen. The columns were made of 10 to 12 drums joined with metal rods. Carving the flutes was started when the drums were on the ground and finished when the column had been raised.

A   B   C

The straight lines of the Parthenon (A) are in fact an optical illusion.

This is how the Parthenon would look without optical corrections (B).

To compensate, it was built with sloping corners and inclining pillars (C).

Builders cut a slot in the top of each stone block opposite a similar slot in the next block, and they poured in molten lead. When the lead hardened, the blocks were held firmly together. No mortar or cement was used.

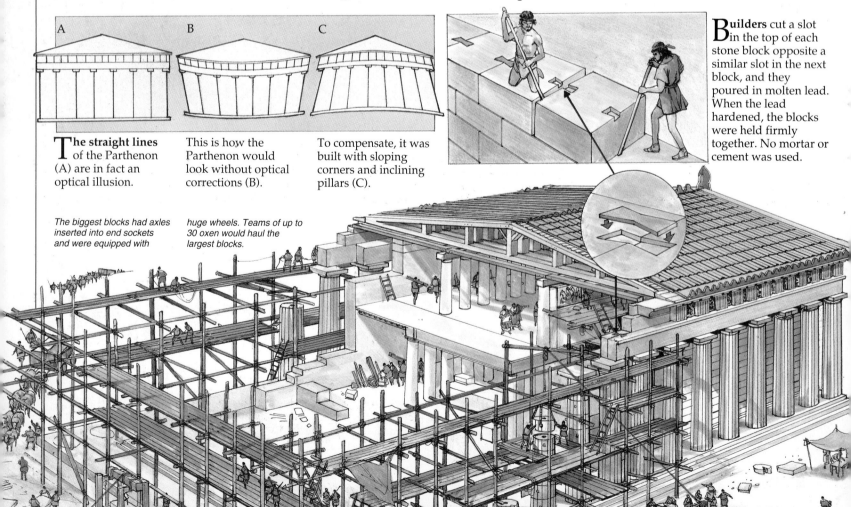

The biggest blocks had axles inserted into end sockets and were equipped with huge wheels. Teams of up to 30 oxen would haul the largest blocks.

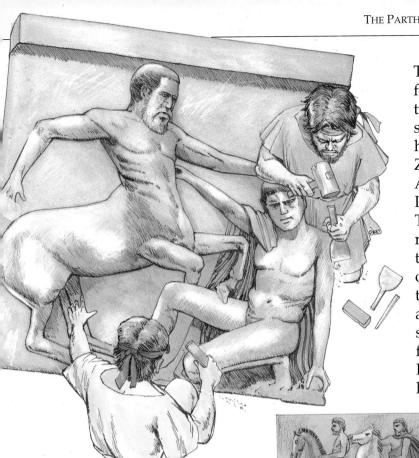

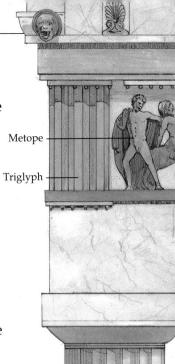

The Parthenon was crowded with figures. In the pediments – the triangular sections at each end – were scenes of Athena's life. One showed her birth from the head of the god Zeus; the other pediment showed Athena's struggle with the god Poseidon for possession of Athens. The 92 metopes – stone blocks with relief sculptures – that surrounded the temple depict scenes of victory over enemies and monsters such as the centaurs, which were half man and half horse. Around the inner section, just below the ceiling, a stone frieze showed scenes from the Great Panathenaia, a special procession held every four years.

Metope

Triglyph

The pediment sculptures were designed by Phidias, but work was carried out by skilled craftsmen. The figures were carved first and then hoisted into position.

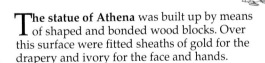
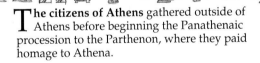

Panels from frieze showing horsemen, Apollo and Poseidon, and a battle.

Athena was adorned with over a ton of gold. The statue cost more than the Parthenon itself.

Athena was sculpted by Phidias.

Athena's golden drapery could be removed in times of danger.

The statue of Athena was 40 feet (12 m) high.

Early in the 5th century A.D., the statue of Athena was carried off to Constantinople.

The statue of Athena was built up by means of shaped and bonded wood blocks. Over this surface were fitted sheaths of gold for the drapery and ivory for the face and hands.

The citizens of Athens gathered outside of Athens before beginning the Panathenaic procession to the Parthenon, where they paid homage to Athena.

In 1687, an attacking Venetian army set off explosives stored in the Parthenon.

In 1801, the occupying Turks authorized Lord Elgin to remove selected sections from the Parthenon. Later sold to the British Museum, they became known as the Elgin Marbles.

A network of corridors and animal pens spread beneath the arena.

There was one entrance for the gladiators, and a small gateway for carrying away dead bodies.

The outside was decorated with arches, pillars and statues.

There were 80 entrances into the Colosseum. Of these, 76 had numbers that corresponded to numbers stamped on spectators' tickets.

Two tall corridors circled the outer edge of the building. Stairways leading from the corridors gave easy access to the seating space. The Colosseum was so well designed that its capacity crowds of 50,000 could get out within minutes.

18

A huge chandelier was suspended above the arena to provide light for nighttime games.

Sailors were posted on the top of the Colosseum to manage the velarium.

THE COLOSSEUM

THE COLOSSEUM, built in the first century A.D., was the largest Roman amphitheater. The development of the arch and vault system and the discovery of concrete enabled Roman architects to design a building of this immense size. But the Colosseum was beautiful as well as imposing. The exterior was encircled with rows of arched arcades, each filled with a statue and framed by columns of white marble. The interior was faced with marble. Yet the sole purpose of this masterpiece of engineering and design was to provide a setting for the cruelest of sports, the gladiator fights. Thousands died in the arena for the entertainment of Colosseum audiences.

In the first century A.D., Rome ruled over a vast empire that included all the land around the Mediterranean sea and most of the rest of Europe. The Roman Empire lasted for over 400 years.

Italy

The Colosseum was built like two Greek theaters joined to form an oval-shaped arena surrounded by rows of tiered seats. But unlike the Greek theater, which was built in a hollow in the earth, the Colosseum had no external supports. Its massive structure was supported by a system of arches and vaults that formed the foundations of the seats.

Below the arena, a maze of passageways led to hundreds of rooms and animal pens. The arena itself could even be flooded to become the setting for mock naval battles.

A huge awning, called a velarium, formed a temporary roof to protect the crowds from sun and rain. It was held up by ropes suspended from 240 poles that encircled the top story.

The colossal statue of Emperor Nero was hauled from his palace using a team of 24 elephants and erected in front of the amphitheater.

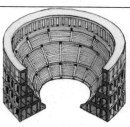

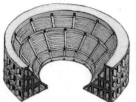

In A.D. 69, Rome lay in ruins after a civil war. Emperor Vespasian began to rebuild the city.

In A.D. 72, a lake in the grounds of Nero's palace was drained. This was the site for the Colosseum.

The concrete foundations were 40 feet (12 m) deep. There were animal pens and rooms underground.

Each story on the outside of the Colosseum was faced with Greek-style columns.

Emperor Vespasian died while the Colosseum was still under construction. His son, Emperor Titus, completed the building in A.D. 80 and celebrated the opening with 100 days of games, which included gladiatorial fights.

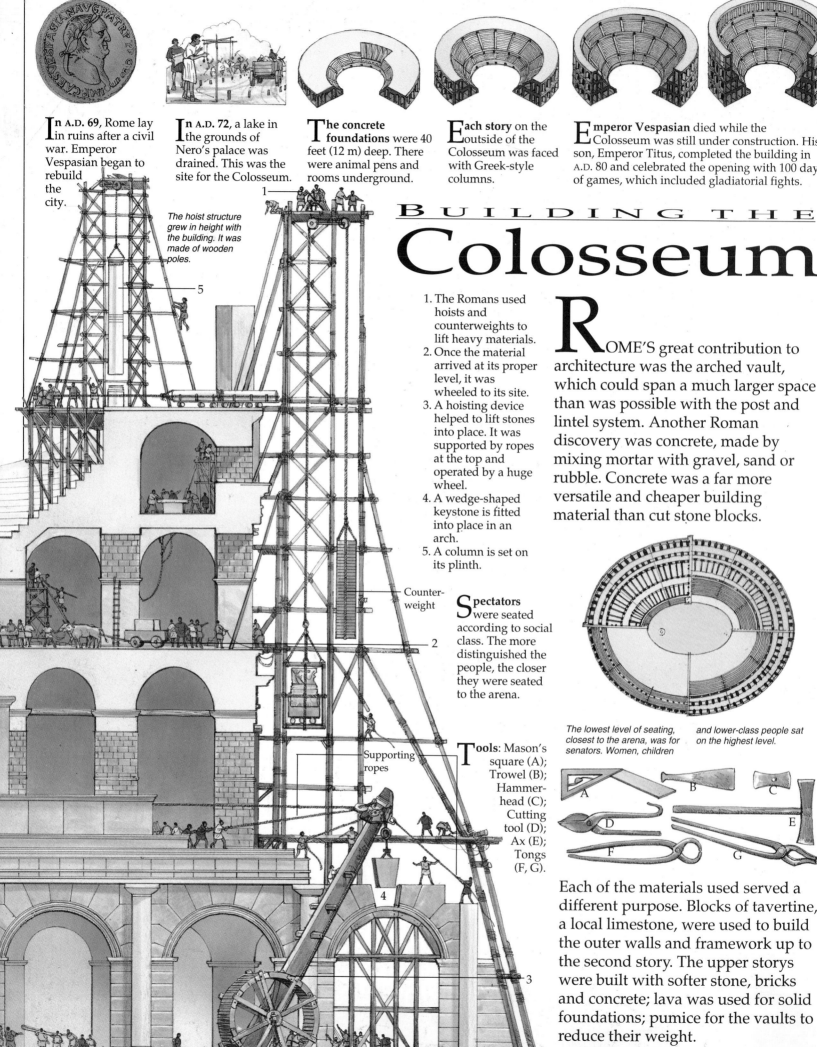

The hoist structure grew in height with the building. It was made of wooden poles.

1. The Romans used hoists and counterweights to lift heavy materials.
2. Once the material arrived at its proper level, it was wheeled to its site.
3. A hoisting device helped to lift stones into place. It was supported by ropes at the top and operated by a huge wheel.
4. A wedge-shaped keystone is fitted into place in an arch.
5. A column is set on its plinth.

Counter-weight

Supporting ropes

BUILDING THE
Colosseum

ROME'S great contribution to architecture was the arched vault, which could span a much larger space than was possible with the post and lintel system. Another Roman discovery was concrete, made by mixing mortar with gravel, sand or rubble. Concrete was a far more versatile and cheaper building material than cut stone blocks.

Spectators were seated according to social class. The more distinguished the people, the closer they were seated to the arena.

The lowest level of seating, closest to the arena, was for senators. Women, children and lower-class people sat on the highest level.

Tools: Mason's square (A); Trowel (B); Hammer-head (C); Cutting tool (D); Ax (E); Tongs (F, G).

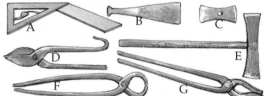

Each of the materials used served a different purpose. Blocks of tavertine, a local limestone, were used to build the outer walls and framework up to the second story. The upper storys were built with softer stone, bricks and concrete; lava was used for solid foundations; pumice for the vaults to reduce their weight.

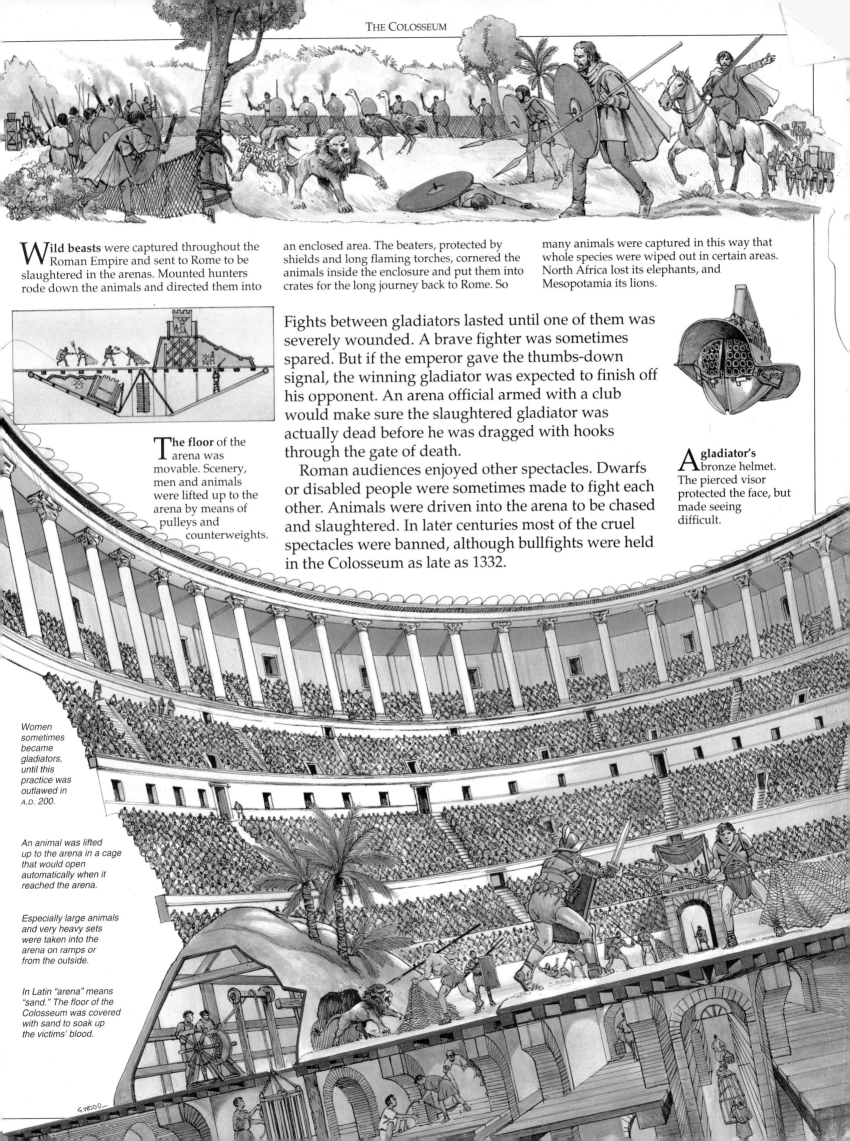

Wild **beasts** were captured throughout the Roman Empire and sent to Rome to be slaughtered in the arenas. Mounted hunters rode down the animals and directed them into an enclosed area. The beaters, protected by shields and long flaming torches, cornered the animals inside the enclosure and put them into crates for the long journey back to Rome. So many animals were captured in this way that whole species were wiped out in certain areas. North Africa lost its elephants, and Mesopotamia its lions.

The **floor** of the arena was movable. Scenery, men and animals were lifted up to the arena by means of pulleys and counterweights.

Fights between gladiators lasted until one of them was severely wounded. A brave fighter was sometimes spared. But if the emperor gave the thumbs-down signal, the winning gladiator was expected to finish off his opponent. An arena official armed with a club would make sure the slaughtered gladiator was actually dead before he was dragged with hooks through the gate of death.

Roman audiences enjoyed other spectacles. Dwarfs or disabled people were sometimes made to fight each other. Animals were driven into the arena to be chased and slaughtered. In later centuries most of the cruel spectacles were banned, although bullfights were held in the Colosseum as late as 1332.

A gladiator's bronze helmet. The pierced visor protected the face, but made seeing difficult.

Women sometimes became gladiators, until this practice was outlawed in A.D. 200.

An animal was lifted up to the arena in a cage that would open automatically when it reached the arena.

Especially large animals and very heavy sets were taken into the arena on ramps or from the outside.

In Latin "arena" means "sand." The floor of the Colosseum was covered with sand to soak up the victims' blood.

G.WOOD

NOTRE DAME

South tower

Clerestory window

TWELFTH-CENTURY Paris was a busy market town that attracted scholars and artists from all over France and Europe. In 1160 a new bishop – Maurice de Sully – inherited a 300-year-old cathedral church that was far too small for the growing population and, with its wooden roof and coarse masonry, hopelessly out-of-date. The new bishop wanted a new cathedral in the Gothic style that was just coming into vogue in France.

Gothic architecture developed from an earlier style known as Romanesque, which had preserved many of the architectural features of Roman times, including round arches and vaults. By the middle of the twelfth century, masons and architects in northern France were experimenting with new building techniques. They learned how to build higher by using pointed arches. They constructed ribbed vaults with pointed arches for the ceiling. The nave of the church was divided into rectangles known as bays. Stone ribs were built along the surface of piers that stood at each corner of the bay. The ribs, which rose to a central point on the ceiling, supported thin stone ceiling panels. As masons became more skilled, ribbing became more elaborately decorated and ceiling vaults were divided into more and more parts. The outward thrust of the high pointed vaults were counterbalanced by stone braces called flying buttresses that reached up from outside supports and pressed against the wall. These three building techniques – pointed arches, ribbed vaults and flying buttresses – formed the new Gothic style of architecture. The Gothic church was higher and its thin walls were pierced with large stained-glass windows.

In 1163 the old cathedral of Paris was demolished to make room for one of the first and perhaps the most beautiful of Gothic cathedrals – Notre Dame.

France

Southern rose window

Paris in the 12th century was an expanding trade center as well as the cultural heart of Europe. The city's population was doubling every generation; by A.D. 1200 it was nearly 100,000. ·

Notre Dame was a vital part of town life. People came here every day to worship or to stroll around the great cathedral, perhaps stopping to listen to a preacher in one of the chapels or to admire the lovely stained-glass windows. These windows, along with the cathedral's carvings and statues, also served as religious instruction at a time when few people could read.

As one of very few public buildings in medieval Paris, Notre Dame served as a place of assembly. It was also a refuge for those in need. Anyone touching the ring of one of the portals was granted the right of sanctuary.

Flying buttress

BUILDING
Notre Dame

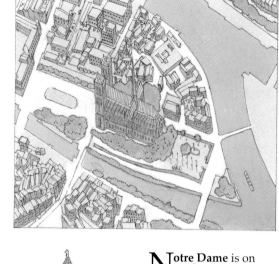

NOTRE DAME WAS A MASTERPIECE of Gothic architecture. The craftsmanship was of rare excellence, even by the standards of the Middle Ages. The cathedral's distinctive western façade is a fine example of the Gothic use of functional decoration. Like an ancient Greek temple, all ornaments are integrated parts of the whole structure.

Notre Dame has a wide nave, double aisles, and small transepts. The choir is surrounded by chapels between the buttresses.

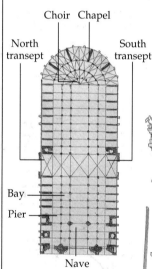

Choir Chapel
North transept   South transept
Bay
Pier
Nave

The niches in the façade were filled with 28 statues, each 10 feet (3 m) tall, representing the kings of Judah. In 1793, during the French Revolution, the crowds, thinking that the Gallery of Kings were images of the French monarchy, pulled down the statues, cut off their heads and threw them in the Seine River.

During both World Wars I and II, the three rose windows were dismantled and stored in safety outside Paris.

Bell tower

Notre Dame is on the Île de la Cité, a small island on the Seine River in the heart of Paris.

The wooden scaffolding was supported by putlogs (horizontal timbers) inserted into the walls. As the walls were built higher, so was the scaffolding. Hundreds of holes are still visible where the putlogs were originally inserted.

A detail of a stained-glass window (above) showing the cancer sign of the zodiac.

The window designers used natural light to enhance the windows' colors. The south rose is predominantly red to reinforce the warm southern sun, while the blues of the northern rose reflect cool northern light. The west rose has the gold tints of evening sunlight.

A lodge close to the cathedral served as a workshop for the architects and stone masons.

Master mason — Architect — Laborers — Master stonecutter — Stone-dresser — Sculptors — Mortar-makers — Stone-carver — Carpenters

There were about 1,000 laborers at work on Notre Dame throughout its construction. The architect and master mason designed the cathedral and supervised its construction. Laborers hauled stone blocks from quarries on the left bank of the Seine.

The master stonecutter chose the best blocks for the purposes they were to serve. Stone-dressers cut the stone into rough shapes for the sculptors. Stone-carvers carved patterns for window frames, doorways and arches. Mortar-makers prepared high-quality mortar, which

was a mixture of sand, quicklime and water. The sand was passed through a sieve to remove pebbles; the lime was exceptionally pure. Carpenters built timber frames to support the arches and windows while they were being built.

Blacksmith — Plumber — Glassblower — Stained-glass glazier

Blacksmiths made iron decorations and repaired building tools. Plumbers coated the roof with sheets of lead. Glassblowers made glass, and craftsmen designed and made the colored stained-glass windows.

The construction of Notre Dame spanned a century. Work began in 1163, and by 1200 the choir, transept and nave were completed and the western façade was under construction. In 1230 the whole top of the church was rebuilt. More windows were added and the clerestory windows were made taller to provide more light. New flying buttresses provided greater stability.

The towers were completed in 1250 and capped with molded cornices. These squared-off towers with no spires were unique in medieval architecture. At this time, the transept was extended by a bay at either end and immense rose windows were built into the north and south façades. Seven chapels were built between the buttresses on either side of the nave. By 1270, exterior work was completed.

Lead roof — Flying buttress — Wooden roof supports — Ribbed vaulting — Buttress — Nave — Aisle — Aisle — Pier — Pointed arch

A Gothic church was characterized by its pointed arches and ribbed vaulting. Heavy stone buttresses were connected by flying buttresses to points on the wall where the vaults exerted the greatest outward thrust. Flying buttresses meant that Gothic architects could build higher, thinner walls, thereby creating space for large stained-glass windows.

Gargoyles are hideous creatures whose mouths spew out the rain runoff.

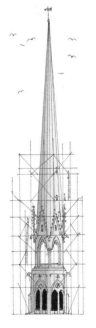

The lead spire was melted to make weapons during the Revolution.

St. Thomas gazing at the spire, which was restored in the mid-1800s.

Notre Dame suffered much abuse over the centuries. Stained glass was removed to let in more light. The portals were mutilated to make room for the canopied litters of French kings. In the mid-1800s, a major restoration project helped to restore Notre Dame to its former grandeur.

Over the centuries Notre Dame has been the setting of several coronations. Henry VI of England was crowned there in 1430; Mary Stuart, Queen of Scots, was crowned Queen of France there upon her marriage to François II in 1558; on December 2, 1804, Napoleon crowned himself Emperor there.

Cathedral of St. John the Divine, New York (begun 1892, still unfinished. Areas in red indicate towers left unbuilt.)

St. Brasilia Cathedral, Brazil (late 1950s)

St. Basil's Cathedral, Moscow (1555-60)

Although the Middle Ages was the great cathedral-building era, magnificent cathedrals have been built up to the present day. The Cathedral of St. John the Divine in New York was begun in 1892 but remains

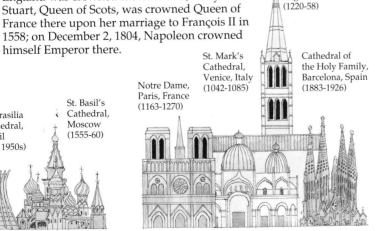

Notre Dame, Paris, France (1163-1270)

St. Mark's Cathedral, Venice, Italy (1042-1085)

Salisbury Cathedral, England (1220-58)

Cathedral of the Holy Family, Barcelona, Spain (1883-1926)

unfinished because the money was used to help the poor. Cologne Cathedral in Germany was built in the Middle Ages, but one spire was added this century. Brasilia, the capital of Brazil, has a very modern-looking cathedral.

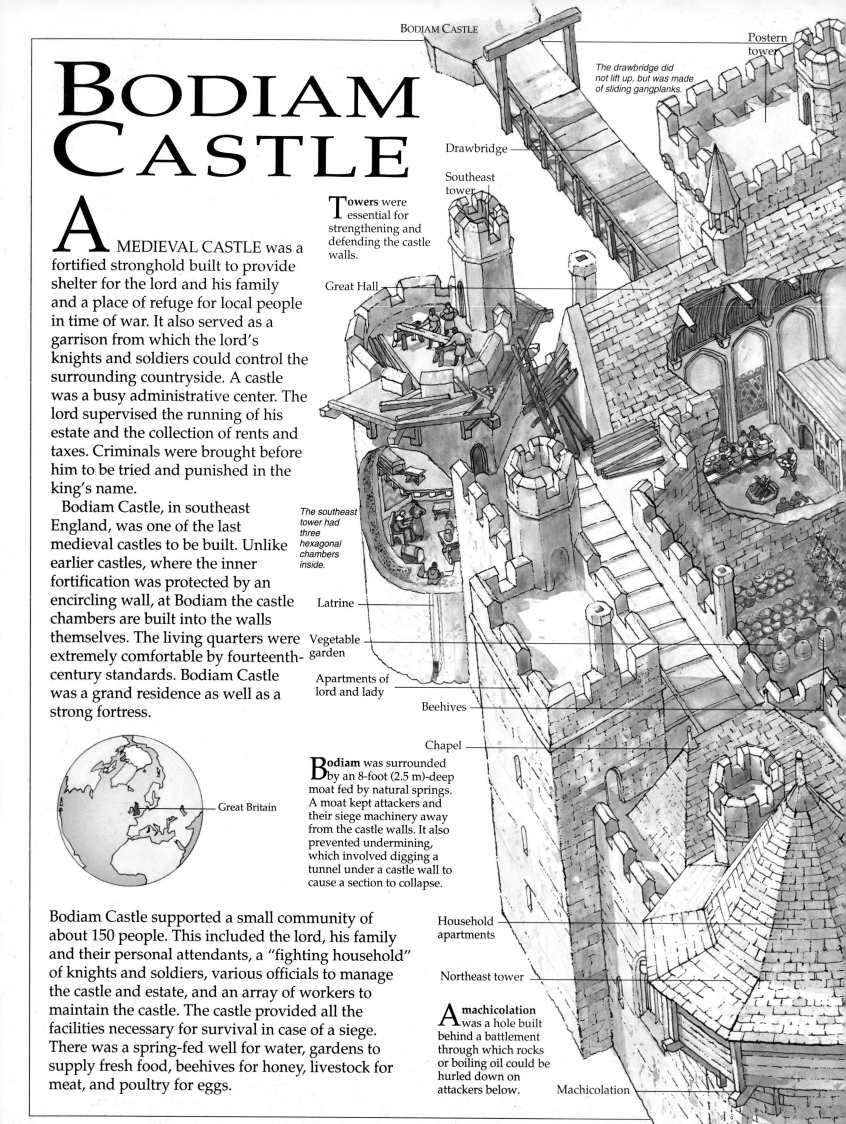

BODIAM CASTLE

A MEDIEVAL CASTLE was a fortified stronghold built to provide shelter for the lord and his family and a place of refuge for local people in time of war. It also served as a garrison from which the lord's knights and soldiers could control the surrounding countryside. A castle was a busy administrative center. The lord supervised the running of his estate and the collection of rents and taxes. Criminals were brought before him to be tried and punished in the king's name.

Bodiam Castle, in southeast England, was one of the last medieval castles to be built. Unlike earlier castles, where the inner fortification was protected by an encircling wall, at Bodiam the castle chambers are built into the walls themselves. The living quarters were extremely comfortable by fourteenth-century standards. Bodiam Castle was a grand residence as well as a strong fortress.

Great Britain

Bodiam Castle supported a small community of about 150 people. This included the lord, his family and their personal attendants, a "fighting household" of knights and soldiers, various officials to manage the castle and estate, and an array of workers to maintain the castle. The castle provided all the facilities necessary for survival in case of a siege. There was a spring-fed well for water, gardens to supply fresh food, beehives for honey, livestock for meat, and poultry for eggs.

The drawbridge did not lift up, but was made of sliding gangplanks.

Postern tower

Drawbridge

Southeast tower

Towers were essential for strengthening and defending the castle walls.

Great Hall

The southeast tower had three hexagonal chambers inside.

Latrine

Vegetable garden

Apartments of lord and lady

Beehives

Chapel

Bodiam was surrounded by an 8-foot (2.5 m)-deep moat fed by natural springs. A moat kept attackers and their siege machinery away from the castle walls. It also prevented undermining, which involved digging a tunnel under a castle wall to cause a section to collapse.

Household apartments

Northeast tower

A machicolation was a hole built behind a battlement through which rocks or boiling oil could be hurled down on attackers below.

Machicolation

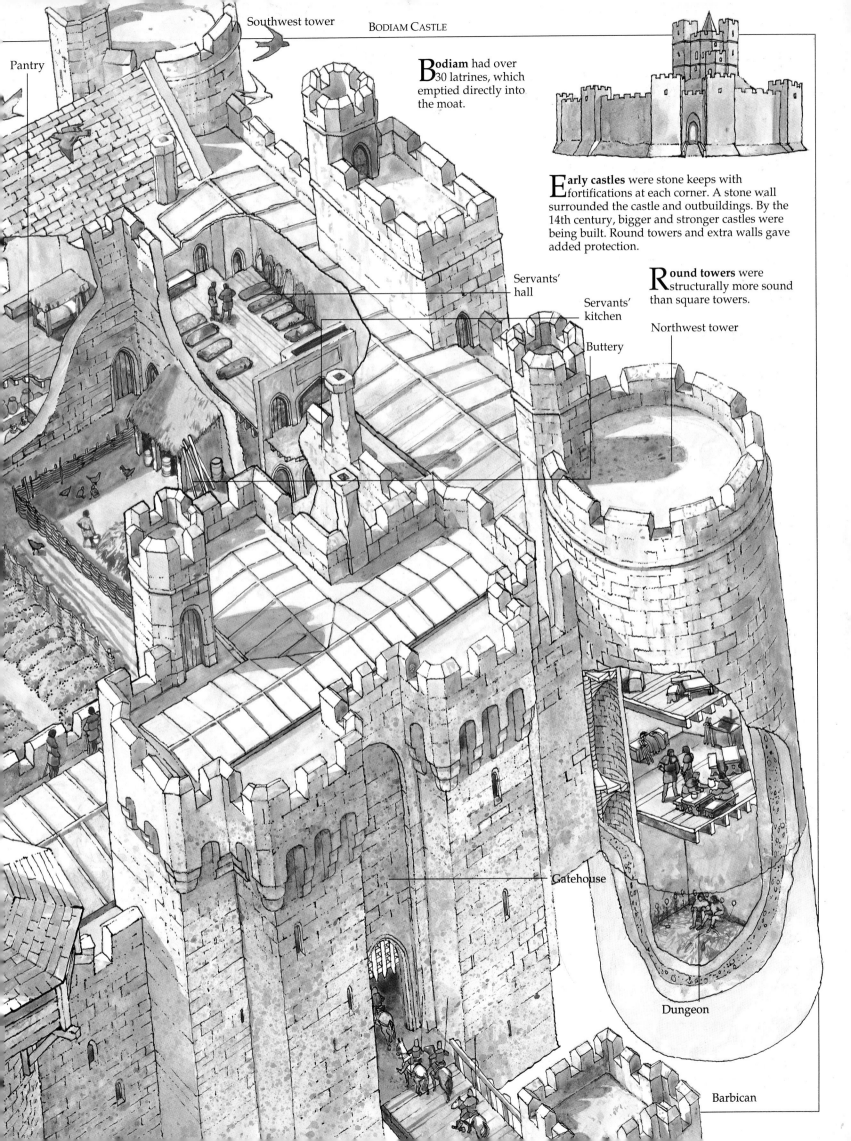

Southwest tower

BODIAM CASTLE

Pantry

Bodiam had over 30 latrines, which emptied directly into the moat.

Early castles were stone keeps with fortifications at each corner. A stone wall surrounded the castle and outbuildings. By the 14th century, bigger and stronger castles were being built. Round towers and extra walls gave added protection.

Servants' hall

Servants' kitchen

Buttery

Round towers were structurally more sound than square towers.

Northwest tower

Gatehouse

Dungeon

Barbican

Sir Edward
Dalyngrigge became rich through plunder during the Hundred Years' War.

In 1377 Sir Edward married Elizabeth Wadeux, who was the heiress to the manor at Bodiam.

The French controlled the English channel from 1372 to 1387, threatening invasion.

In 1385 Richard II granted a license to fortify Bodiam manor. Sir Edward built a new castle.

In 1387 the English gained control of the Channel, before work on the castle had been completed.

In 1483, the castle surrendered to the Earl of Surrey, who acted on the authority of Richard III.

B U I L D I N G
Bodiam Castle

THE ARCHITECTURAL INNOVATIONS and masonry skills developed in the construction of cathedrals were applied to the thousands of castles built throughout Europe during the Middle Ages. Bodiam Castle incorporated the most up-to-date features of castle design. Master craftsmen recruited from all over Europe produced a castle that was an impenetrable fortress and a luxurious residence.

The castle walls were made of massive stone blocks, 6 feet (2 m) thick on average, which were either brought by barge down the Rother River or hauled 12 miles (19 km) overland. Oak from the Ashdown Forest was used for rafters, joists, flooring and paneling.

Murder holes in the gatehouse ceilings were used to drop rocks or stakes on attackers below.

The gunloops in both gatehouses were used for firing cannon.

A spring-fed well provided water for the castle. It was boiled and made into beer before drinking.

Castle-building was supervised by a master stonemason.

Frame saw (1); Anvil hammer (2); Saw (3); Mallet (4); Plane (5).

Each team of workers was supervised by a master craftsman.

Scaffolding was made from wooden poles tied together with rope.

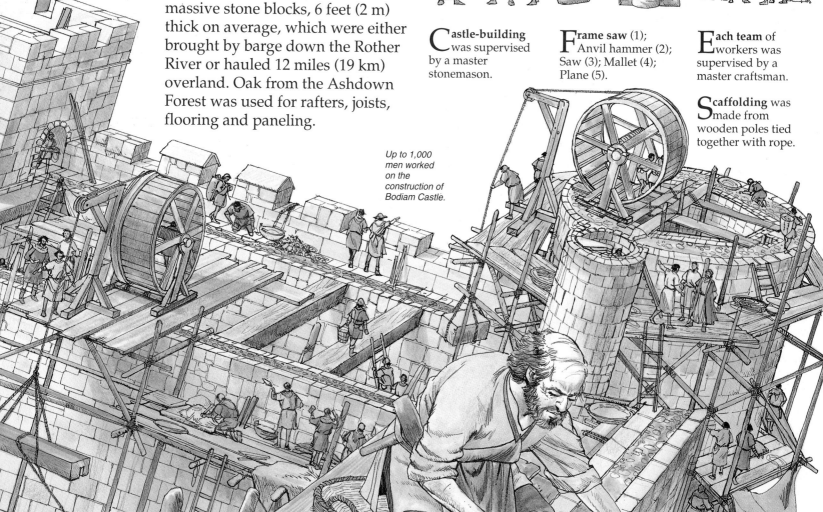

Up to 1,000 men worked on the construction of Bodiam Castle.

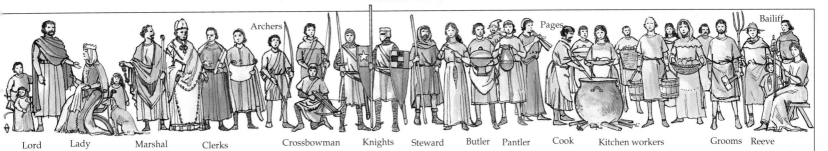

BODIAM CASTLE

Lord Lady Marshal Clerks Archers Crossbowman Knights Steward Butler Pantler Cook Kitchen workers Pages Grooms Reeve Bailiff

A castle supported a whole community of people who served the lord and lady. The marshal, helped by grooms, pages and serving maids, organized the castle lodgings.

The butler and pantler were responsible for buying and storing food. The ewerer provided clean cloths for the lord's table. The cook and kitchen workers prepared meals for the castle household. The steward ran the lord's estate; clerks kept accounts, and a reeve and bailiff collected farm rents. Knights, archers and crossbowmen guarded the castle.

The lord's apartment was in the east wing.

The castle guards kept watch from the towers.

The great hall was one of the most important rooms in any castle. It was here that the castle household gathered for meals and to celebrate feasts. The lord and his family and guests sat apart from the rest of the household, at a high table placed crossways on a raised platform. Often the lord and his family would dine in the privacy of their own apartments. These rooms, with their fireplaces and adjoining latrines, were the most luxurious accommodation in the castle.

The pigeon loft in the southwest tower had about 300 nesting boxes. Keeping pigeons and doves was the right of the lord of the manor, although local farmers resented the birds eating their crops. Pigeons provided eggs and food for the castle household.

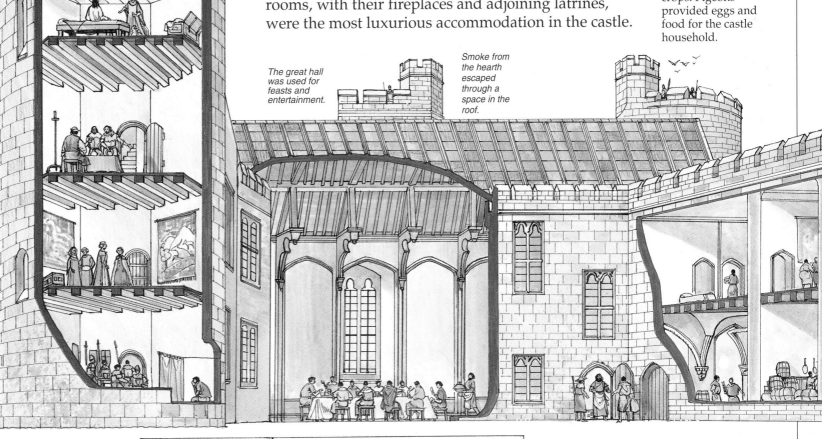

The great hall was used for feasts and entertainment.

Smoke from the hearth escaped through a space in the roof.

Although castles were made obsolete by improvements in firearms, many "bogus" castles were erected in later centuries as splendid residences, not as fortresses. Schloss Neuschwanstein in Germany is a bogus castle built for King Ludwig II of Bavaria in the 19th century. Its design is similar to many medieval European castles.

By the end of the fourteenth century, when cannon had become powerful enough to crumble solid stone walls, the castle had become obsolete as a fortress. But the castle's influence could still be seen in the design of large courtyard houses, with their towers, battlements and even moats.

Bodiam Castle was occupied until the English Civil War (1640-48), when it was burned. It lay in ruins until 1916, when restoration was begun. The outer walls still stand today.

MONT ST. MICHEL

Mont St. Michel is an island just off the coast of Normandy in France.

France

Most monasteries consisted of a group of buildings surrounding a church. At Mont St. Michel, the church is perched on the top of the island, and the rest of the monastery buildings are piled one on top of the other along the sides of the island.

The monastery, built into the side of the hill, was such an amazing architectural accomplishment that it became known as *la Merveille* – the Marvel.

The church of Mont St. Michel is supported on a summit that is one-quarter of its size. The two monasteries built to serve the church cling to the north and west sides of the rocky cliffs. Their upper chambers are at the level of the church floor. Some of the great halls of the older monastery, which dates back to the eleventh century, have fallen away. The thirteenth-century monastery on the north side of the island forms a single vertical wall rising 133 feet (40 m) from the bedrock below.

A small town grew up at the foot of the monastery to accommodate the pilgrims.

The foundation of the church of Mont St. Michel is 245 feet (73.5 m) above sea level.

Mont St. Michel has been a place of pilgrimage since the eighth century. In the eleventh century, a group of Benedictine monks arrived and began to build a church on the very summit of the island. Only the transept of the church rests on a solid rock base; the rest of the structure is supported by massive foundations built up on all four sides. Over the next five centuries the church and monastery that served it were extended, enlarged and rebuilt until most of the island was covered with buildings.

In 1048, William the Conqueror and Harold the Saxon visited Mont St. Michel. Harold rescued several soldiers from the quicksands.

Pilgrims traveled to Mont St. Michel to seek the blessing of Michael the Archangel. The pilgrims were known as *Miquelots* after their patron, Michael.

Pilgrims arrived by boat when the tides were in. At low tide they crossed the ribbon of land that connected Mont St. Michel to the mainland. They were led by islanders who guided them around the invisible quicksand.

According to legend, in A.D. 709 Michael the Archangel appeared to the Bishop of Avranches and ordered him to build a shrine in the Scissy Forest on the Normandy coast.

Over the years the sea flooded the forest, and twice a day the hill became an island. In 950, a church was built to serve the growing number of pilgrims.

In 1020, Benedictine monks came to the island and began work on an abbey church on the summit of the hill. Foundations were built out on all four sides to support the church walls.

BUILDING
Mont St. Michel

THE THIRTEENTH-CENTURY monastery known as *la Merveille* was built in splendid Gothic style with pointed arches and vaulted ceilings. Each vaulted room served as a foundation for another more delicately vaulted and lighter room above. The kitchen and storerooms were on the lowest level because all supplies including water had to be hauled up by treadmill. There was also an almsroom where the monks dispensed charity to the poor who came begging. On the second floor was the great hall. Next to it was the scriptorium, where the monks copied and illuminated books for the monastery library. The third floor opened out into the transept of the church. Here were the monks' refectory and dormitories.

In the Middle Ages monasteries served as inns for travelers, hospitals for the sick, and places of refuge for the poor.

Monks' refectory

Great Hall

Alms Hall

Buttress

Michael the Archangel, patron of warriors, defeated Satan and expelled him from heaven.

In the 11th century Benedictine monks came to Mont St. Michel. They established a library that became famous throughout Europe.

Life in the monastery was regulated by the Rule of St. Benedict.

The monks' day lasted from sunrise to sunset, and was divided into 12 equal hours. The amount of time the monks spent on each activity varied as the seasons changed.

Cloister

Church transept

During the Hundred Years' War between France and England, ramparts were built to encircle the island.

Storeroom

Scriptorium

The monks said prayers 7 times a day.

They ate in silence while a fellow monk read to them.

Monks copied out and illuminated the Bible.

A monk's duties included cleaning the monastery.

Evening was a time for meditation and rest in the cloister.

A monk's sleep was interrupted for prayers.

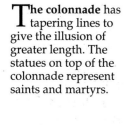

The colonnade has tapering lines to give the illusion of greater length. The statues on top of the colonnade represent saints and martyrs.

The obelisk, originally from Egypt, once stood in Nero's Circus. It was moved to the piazza in 1586.

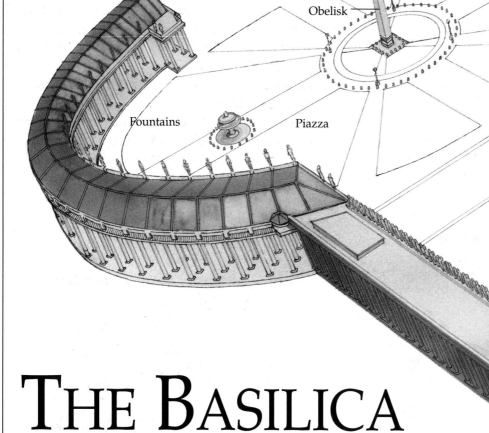

Colonnade

Obelisk

Fountains

Piazza

THE BASILICA OF ST. PETER

THE BASILICA OF ST. PETER in Rome, one of the most magnificent churches ever built, represents the finest example of Italian Renaissance architecture. The Renaissance refers to the "rebirth" of the art and writing of the Classical Age (400 B.C. to A.D. 400), which was the time of the Greek and Roman empires. The creative spirit of the Renaissance began in Italy in the early fifteenth century and soon spread to the rest of Europe. Renaissance architecture was characterized by a return to classical forms such as Greek and Roman columns. The main features of a Renaissance church were an exterior dome and semicircular Roman arches and vaults, which replaced the Gothic pointed arches and ribbed vaults.

The Basilica of St. Peter and the Sistine Chapel are located in Vatican City, a walled city on the west bank of the Tiber River in Rome. An independent city-state covering 110 acres (44 ha), it has been the main residence of the Pope since 1377, although popes are said to have lived there as early as the 5th century A.D. Vatican City achieved full independence from Italy in 1929.

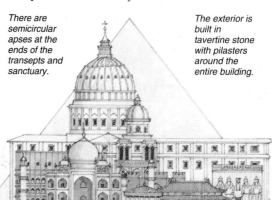

There are semicircular apses at the ends of the transepts and sanctuary.

The exterior is built in tavertine stone with pilasters around the entire building.

The nave is flanked by piers 75 feet (25 m) high and entablatures 20 feet (6 m) high.

The interior walls are of brick faced with plaster colored to imitate marble.

St. Peter's, the world's largest church, is 710 feet (213 m) long and 456 feet (137 m) across the bay, and can hold up to 50,000 people. It is more than twice the size of Notre Dame.

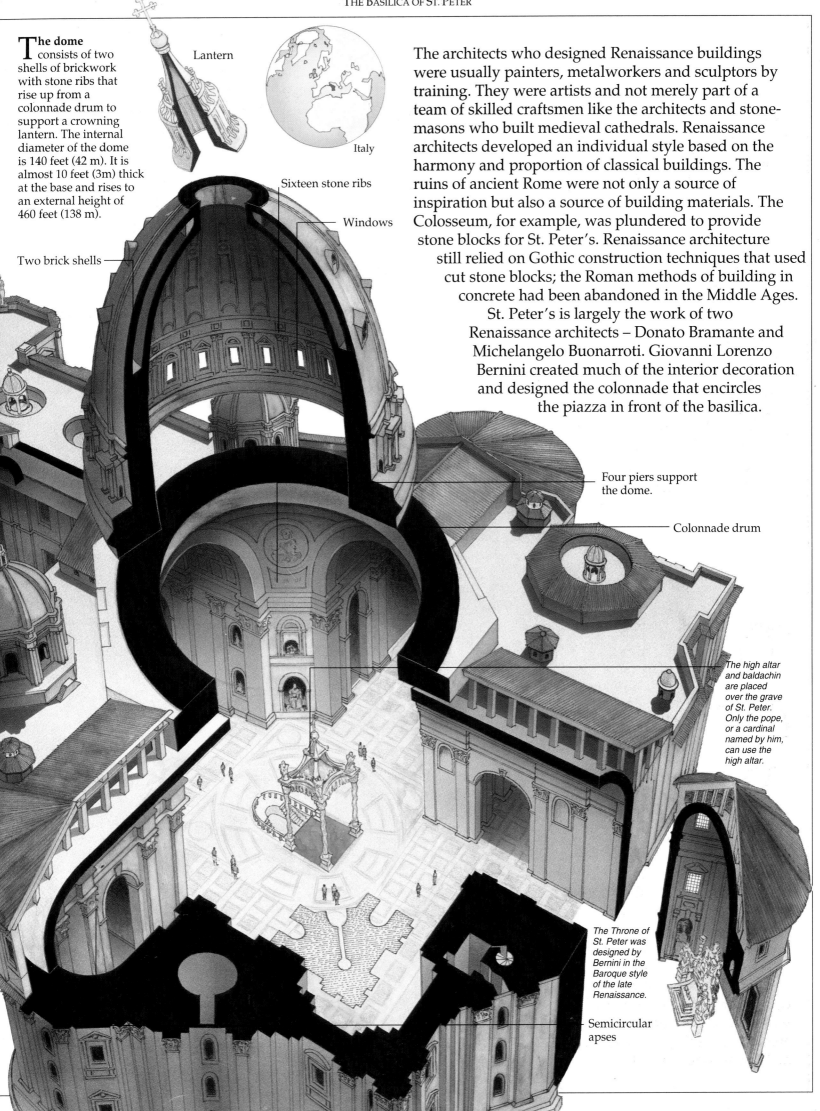

The dome consists of two shells of brickwork with stone ribs that rise up from a colonnade drum to support a crowning lantern. The internal diameter of the dome is 140 feet (42 m). It is almost 10 feet (3m) thick at the base and rises to an external height of 460 feet (138 m).

Lantern

Italy

Sixteen stone ribs

Windows

Two brick shells

The architects who designed Renaissance buildings were usually painters, metalworkers and sculptors by training. They were artists and not merely part of a team of skilled craftsmen like the architects and stone-masons who built medieval cathedrals. Renaissance architects developed an individual style based on the harmony and proportion of classical buildings. The ruins of ancient Rome were not only a source of inspiration but also a source of building materials. The Colosseum, for example, was plundered to provide stone blocks for St. Peter's. Renaissance architecture still relied on Gothic construction techniques that used cut stone blocks; the Roman methods of building in concrete had been abandoned in the Middle Ages. St. Peter's is largely the work of two Renaissance architects – Donato Bramante and Michelangelo Buonarroti. Giovanni Lorenzo Bernini created much of the interior decoration and designed the colonnade that encircles the piazza in front of the basilica.

Four piers support the dome.

Colonnade drum

The high altar and baldachin are placed over the grave of St. Peter. Only the pope, or a cardinal named by him, can use the high altar.

The Throne of St. Peter was designed by Bernini in the Baroque style of the late Renaissance.

Semicircular apses

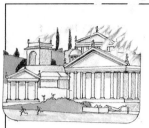

In A.D. 64, a fire destroyed half of Rome. Emperor Nero blamed the Christians and had them killed.

Many Christians were crucified. Among them was St. Peter, an apostle of Christ.

Peter asked to be crucified upside down because he felt unworthy to die the same way as Christ.

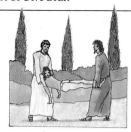

St. Peter's disciples buried his body in a cemetery on Vatican Hill close to Nero's Circus.

Christianity spread, and in A.D. 160 a shrine was built to mark St. Peter's grave.

In A.D. 312, Emperor Constantine made Christianity lawful and built a basilica over the shrine.

BUILDING
St. Peter's
AND THE Sistine Chapel

THE ORIGINAL ST. PETER'S had stood for more than 1,100 years when Pope Julius II had it demolished to make room for a new basilica. The foundation stone was laid in 1506 and the new church was consecrated 120 years later in 1626. The first architect was Donato Bramante, who designed the church in the form of a Greek cross under a dome. Bramante died in 1514 and was succeeded by a number of architects over the next 32 years, each with ideas of his own that differed from the original plan. In 1546 Michelangelo Buonarroti, then 72 years old, was called in as architect. He was given complete freedom to make changes. Michelangelo restored Bramante's original Greek cross plan and designed a dome. After Michelangelo's death in 1564, his plans for the dome were carried out, but the floor plan and façade were changed. The nave was lengthened to form a Latin cross, which obscured the view of the dome from the Piazza.

The altar was placed above the grave of St. Peter. Pilgrims came from all over Europe to visit this holy place. Buildings grew up around the basilica to house the pilgrims.

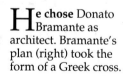

The foundation medal for the new St. Peter's cast in 1506 shows Bramante's original design with a vast central dome. Four smaller domes are set above the arms of the Greek cross.

In 1506, Pope Julius II had the old basilica torn down to make room for a new church.

He chose Donato Bramante as architect. Bramante's plan (right) took the form of a Greek cross.

Giovanni Lorenzo Bernini, painter, sculptor and architect, took nine years (1633-1642) to create the 97-foot (29 m)-tall baldachin (left) over the high altar. The bronze canopy is supported by four columns of bronze. Bernini also designed the grand colonnade.

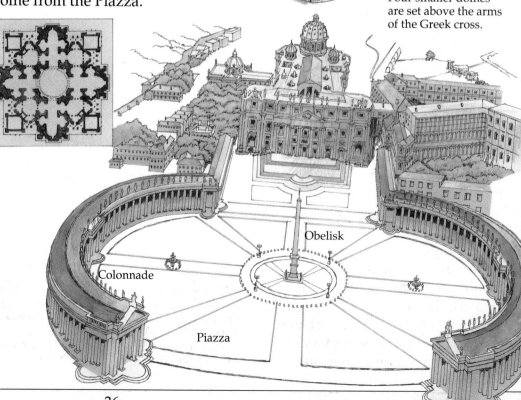

Colonnade

Obelisk

Piazza

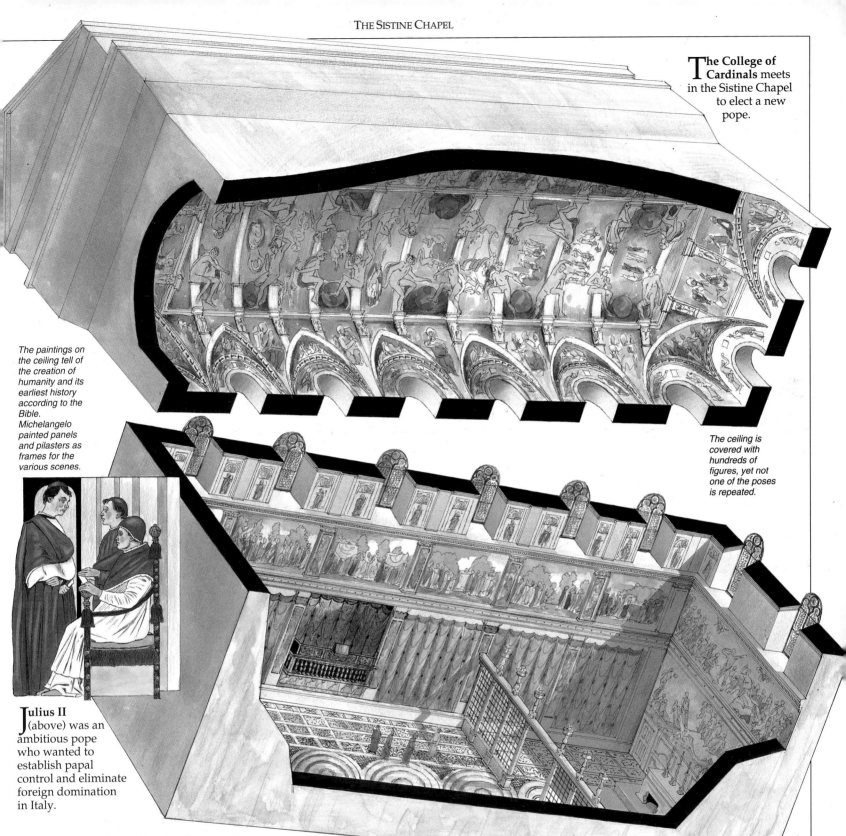

The College of Cardinals meets in the Sistine Chapel to elect a new pope.

The paintings on the ceiling tell of the creation of humanity and its earliest history according to the Bible. Michelangelo painted panels and pilasters as frames for the various scenes.

The ceiling is covered with hundreds of figures, yet not one of the poses is repeated.

Julius II (above) was an ambitious pope who wanted to establish papal control and eliminate foreign domination in Italy.

The Sistine Chapel, which stands next to St. Peter's, is the pope's private chapel. It was built between 1473 and 1481 for Pope Sixtus IV. Pope Julius II commissioned Michelangelo Buonarroti to paint its 87-foot (26 m)-high ceiling. Many of Michelangelo's rivals thought his lack of experience in fresco painting would reflect poorly on his skill as an artist. However, many people consider the ceiling of the Sistine Chapel to be the greatest work of art ever created by one person.

The fresco technique was used to paint the Sistine Chapel. First the plasterer troweled a smooth layer of thin, wet plaster over a layer of dry plaster.

Next an assistant tacked up a piece of paper with a line drawing of the figure that was to be painted. Holes had been pierced along the lines of the figures.

He then tapped along the holes with a porous bag of charcoal dust. When the paper was removed, a charcoal dust outline of the figure was left behind.

An artist painted on the wet plaster. As it dried, pigments from the water-based paint became bound in the plaster and the colors lightened.

THE TAJ MAHAL

India

THE TAJ MAHAL near Agra in India, considered by many to be the greatest work of architecture of all times, was inspired by love and grief. In 1631 Shah Jahan, a Moghul emperor of India, was heartbroken at the death of his wife, known as Mumtaz Mahal, "Chosen One of the Palace." He wanted the mausoleum where Mumtaz would be laid to rest to be more beautiful than anything ever built. The white marble tomb became known by another version of his wife's title – Taj Mahal, the "Crown of the Palace."

Outer dome

Inner dome

White marble facing

Rubble

Underground tombs

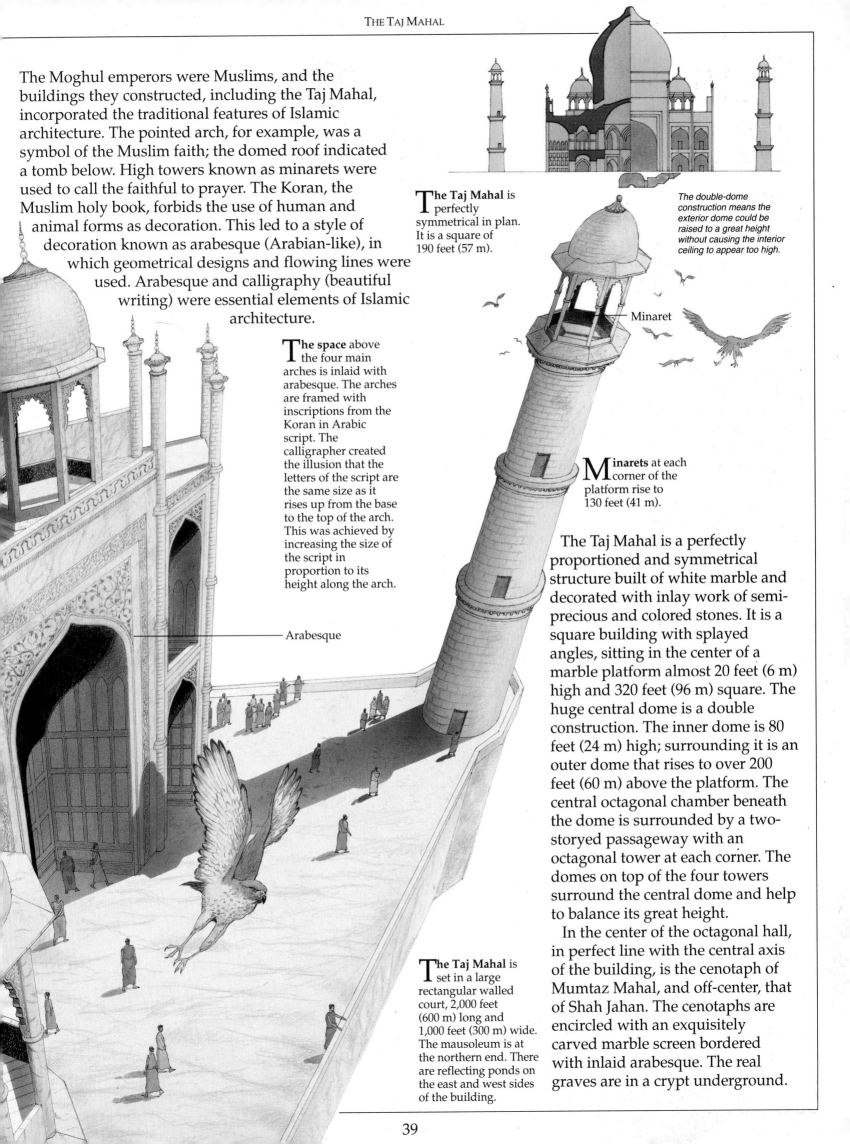

The Moghul emperors were Muslims, and the buildings they constructed, including the Taj Mahal, incorporated the traditional features of Islamic architecture. The pointed arch, for example, was a symbol of the Muslim faith; the domed roof indicated a tomb below. High towers known as minarets were used to call the faithful to prayer. The Koran, the Muslim holy book, forbids the use of human and animal forms as decoration. This led to a style of decoration known as arabesque (Arabian-like), in which geometrical designs and flowing lines were used. Arabesque and calligraphy (beautiful writing) were essential elements of Islamic architecture.

The Taj Mahal is perfectly symmetrical in plan. It is a square of 190 feet (57 m).

The double-dome construction means the exterior dome could be raised to a great height without causing the interior ceiling to appear too high.

— Minaret

The space above the four main arches is inlaid with arabesque. The arches are framed with inscriptions from the Koran in Arabic script. The calligrapher created the illusion that the letters of the script are the same size as it rises up from the base to the top of the arch. This was achieved by increasing the size of the script in proportion to its height along the arch.

Minarets at each corner of the platform rise to 130 feet (41 m).

— Arabesque

The Taj Mahal is a perfectly proportioned and symmetrical structure built of white marble and decorated with inlay work of semi-precious and colored stones. It is a square building with splayed angles, sitting in the center of a marble platform almost 20 feet (6 m) high and 320 feet (96 m) square. The huge central dome is a double construction. The inner dome is 80 feet (24 m) high; surrounding it is an outer dome that rises to over 200 feet (60 m) above the platform. The central octagonal chamber beneath the dome is surrounded by a two-storyed passageway with an octagonal tower at each corner. The domes on top of the four towers surround the central dome and help to balance its great height.

In the center of the octagonal hall, in perfect line with the central axis of the building, is the cenotaph of Mumtaz Mahal, and off-center, that of Shah Jahan. The cenotaphs are encircled with an exquisitely carved marble screen bordered with inlaid arabesque. The real graves are in a crypt underground.

The Taj Mahal is set in a large rectangular walled court, 2,000 feet (600 m) long and 1,000 feet (300 m) wide. The mausoleum is at the northern end. There are reflecting ponds on the east and west sides of the building.

BUILDING THE
Taj Mahal

SHAH JAHAN decided to build his wife a mausoleum that would be unsurpassed for its beauty. Architects from all over the east competed for the honor of designing the perfect tomb. The plan that finally won Shah Jahan's approval undoubtedly included many of his own ideas.

In 1526 the Moghuls founded an empire in India. By 1707, their empire (shown in yellow) covered most of India.

Shah Jahan, heir to the throne of the Moghul empire, was born in 1592.

Shah Jahan was given the best of education and developed a particular interest in architecture. By the time he was 15, Jahan was being asked to remodel old palaces and design parts of new ones.

The white marble of the Taj Mahal is only a veneer. The building was actually made of rubble and faced with marble.

The women of the court shopped at a private market. Men were allowed in only on special days.

Shah Jahan saw Mumtaz and fell instantly in love. He asked his father for Mumtaz as his wife.

Then, princes married for political reasons. But Jahan was allowed to marry Mumtaz.

In 1627 Shah Jahan became emperor. The jewel-encrusted peacock throne displayed his wealth.

Mumtaz even went to war with Jahan. She died after giving birth to their 14th child.

The Jamuna River was diverted to the foot of the foundations so that the view from the completed tomb would be improved.

A 10-mile (16 km) ramp of trampled earth was laid through Agra for the transport of material. Elephants dragged blocks of marble to the building site.

The Moghul rulers built many domed mausoleums. Some served as models for the Taj Mahal.

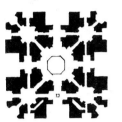

The central chamber is linked by radiating passages to the octagonal rooms at each corner.

This shows the arabesque on the marble screen in the central chamber.

Shah Jahan attracted many first-class craftsmen and artists from all over his empire and beyond to work on the Taj Mahal. The team of artisans included an engineer to build the domes, workers of precious metals, designers, stonecutters, masons, carvers and inlayers. The master calligrapher ranked as high as the architect and was the only artisan whose signature appears on the walls of the Taj Mahal.

The mausoleum took ten years to complete, but the entire complex took another twelve years. Over twenty thousand people were employed at the site throughout the twenty-two years. A city, known as Mumtazbad, grew up to house the workers.

The Gol Gombaz at Bijapur is the mausoleum of Sultan Muhammad Adil Shah (1626-56). It contains one of the largest domes in the world.

In 1642, the year the mausoleum was finished, Shah Jahan held an elaborate memorial service. Mumtaz Mahal's body was finally laid to rest in the world's most beautiful tomb.

In 1658 Shah Jahan fell ill, and his third son, who took control of the empire, had his father imprisoned at the Agra Fort, where he could gaze down the river to the Taj Mahal. Shah Jahan died in 1666 and was buried beside Mumtaz Mahal.

THE FORBIDDEN CITY

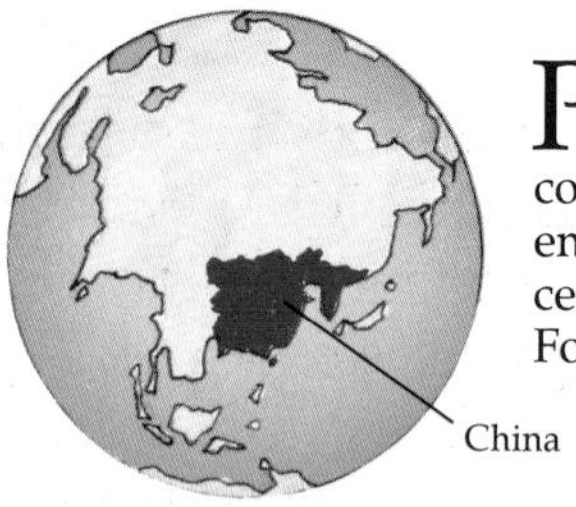

Peking was made up of three concentric walled enclosures. At the center was the Forbidden City.

China

THE FORBIDDEN CITY was the imperial palace for generations of Chinese emperors. Here the emperor lived in luxury and seclusion in a royal city that was forbidden on pain of death to most of his subjects.

The imperial palace was a complex of audience halls and residences, connected by courtyards. The Chinese were not interested in building lasting monuments or magnificent palaces like those built for European monarchs. Instead, Chinese architecture sought to reflect the dynamic balance of opposing forces within nature (the yin and yang), which was an important part of Chinese spiritual beliefs.

The emperor of China was considered by his subjects to be the "Son of Heaven" around whom everything on earth revolved. It was the emperor's role as the source of power and stability to stand at the center of the world and control everything. For the ancient Chinese, the Forbidden City at the center of Peking represented the center of the world.

The roof tiles were very thick and semicircular.

The Forbidden City was rectangular, 3,350 feet (1,005 m) by 2,526 feet (758 m), surrounded by a moat.

Meridian Gate

42

The emphasis was on the relationship of the buildings to each other and to the landscape. Each building in the Forbidden City was separate yet integrated into an overall design. Over the centuries many of the palace's wooden buildings were destroyed by fire and had to be rebuilt, but always following the same basic architectural and design principles.

The Forbidden City was laid out in a rectangular grid pattern with a north-south axis, facing the sunny south. The two main gates were aligned on the north-south axis, which extended beyond the walls of the Forbidden City and formed the principal axis of the imperial city and Peking. Each building was positioned according to its function and status.

The Meridian Gate, the southern entrance, consisted of a 200-foot (60 m)-long pavilion flanked by two square pavilions and raised on a marble platform 50 feet (15 m) high.

The Meridian Gate was reserved for the use of the emperor alone. The striking of drums and sounding of bells from the towers above announced his departure through the gate and also marked his ascending the throne within the palace for one of the state ceremonies.

Hall of Supreme Harmony

Courtyard

Many buildings were decorated with colorful glazed tiles and ceramic ornaments.

Supreme Imperial Gate

The marble balustrades and central ramps leading to the Hall of Supreme Harmony were carved with dragons, the symbol of the emperor.

Color was used to differentiate the three architectural elements of the buildings. Platforms were white; pillars and walls were red; and roof tiles were yellow, the color reserved for the emperor.

Charcoal-burning stoves were placed outside the buildings in a sort of ditch. Pipes from the stoves ran under the bricks of the floor to heat the inside of the buildings.

The River of Golden Water was spanned by five marble bridges. Only the emperor used the central bridge.

Central Bridge

River of Golden Water

In the courtyard before the Hall of Supreme Harmony rows of court officials would take up their positions according to rank with the help of bronze markers set in the ground. They would prostrate themselves nine times when the emperor ascended the throne.

In 1211 the Mongols, led by Genghis Khan, first invaded China and set up the Mongol Dynasty.

Kublai Khan, his grandson, completed the conquest and set up the Yuan Dynasty.

Kublai Khan built the Forbidden City; around it was the imperial city, with Peking outside that.

In 1368 the Mongols were driven out of China. The new Ming emperor ordered the destruction of the Forbidden City. In 1404 the second Ming emperor began to re-build the imperial palace.

The Qing dynasty took over in 1644. The Forbidden City sustained damage, but was later restored.

BUILDING THE
Forbidden City

THE MOST STRIKING FEATURE of Chinese buildings was the curved roof. This was achieved by using rectangular roof trusses. Unlike the triangular truss used in European architecture, the Chinese system allowed shallow curves in the roof by varying the lengths of the crossbeams.

Chinese building procedures were the reverse of those used in most other countries. Instead of raising the columns and framing the rest of the building on them, the Chinese first made the framework of the roof and this determined the positions of the columns. The walls were merely screens and not used for support.

When a court official reported to the emperor, he was expected to kowtow, which involved three kneelings and nine prostrations, some distance away from the throne. A violation of court etiquette could result in an immediate beating. In later reigns, violations were sometimes punished by death.

Hall of Supreme Harmony

Cantilevered brackets at the end of the columns enabled the edge of the roof to be extended outward, well beyond the line of the pillars.

A detail of the Dragon Pavement (below).

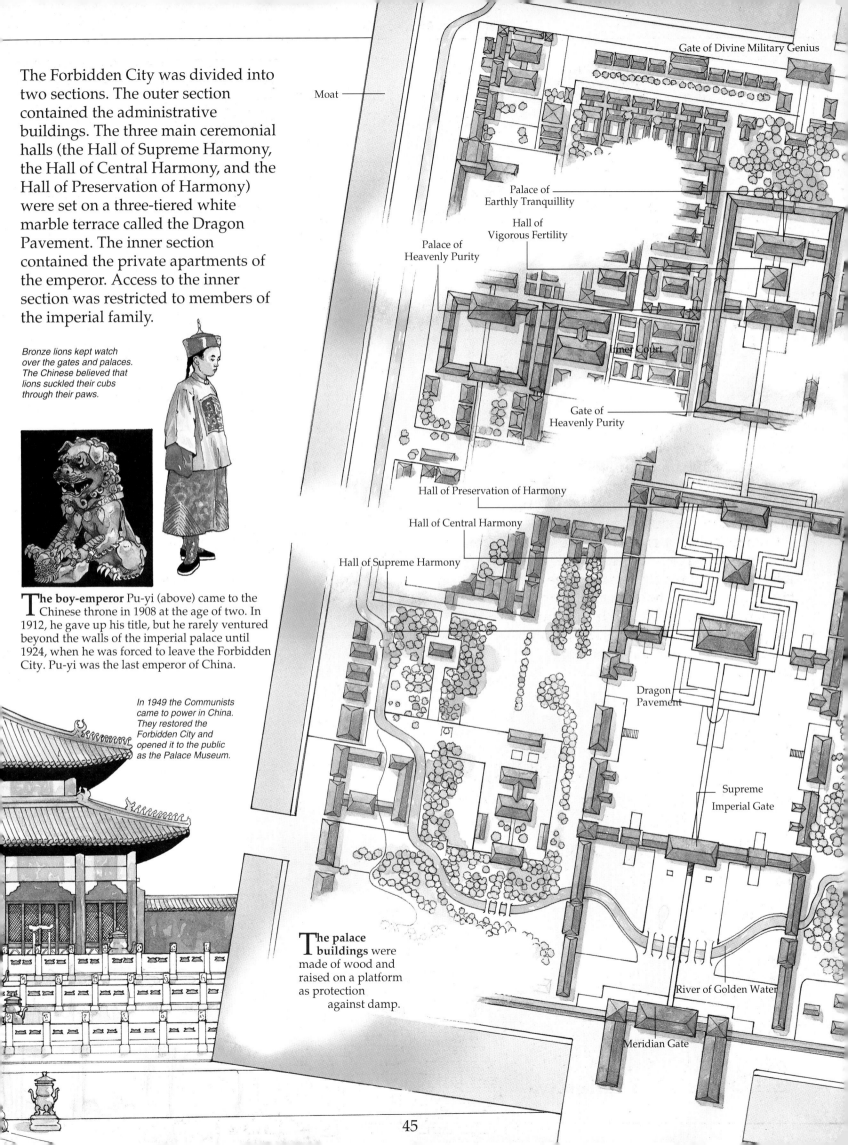

The Forbidden City was divided into two sections. The outer section contained the administrative buildings. The three main ceremonial halls (the Hall of Supreme Harmony, the Hall of Central Harmony, and the Hall of Preservation of Harmony) were set on a three-tiered white marble terrace called the Dragon Pavement. The inner section contained the private apartments of the emperor. Access to the inner section was restricted to members of the imperial family.

Bronze lions kept watch over the gates and palaces. The Chinese believed that lions suckled their cubs through their paws.

The boy-emperor Pu-yi (above) came to the Chinese throne in 1908 at the age of two. In 1912, he gave up his title, but he rarely ventured beyond the walls of the imperial palace until 1924, when he was forced to leave the Forbidden City. Pu-yi was the last emperor of China.

In 1949 the Communists came to power in China. They restored the Forbidden City and opened it to the public as the Palace Museum.

The palace **buildings** were made of wood and raised on a platform as protection against damp.

Gate of Divine Military Genius

Moat

Palace of Earthly Tranquillity

Hall of Vigorous Fertility

Palace of Heavenly Purity

Inner Court

Gate of Heavenly Purity

Hall of Preservation of Harmony

Hall of Central Harmony

Hall of Supreme Harmony

Dragon Pavement

Supreme Imperial Gate

River of Golden Water

Meridian Gate

THE X-RAY PICTURE BOOK OF BIG BUILDINGS OF THE ANCIENT WORLD GLOSSARY

Acropolis The upper part of an ancient Greek city where the main temples and monuments were built. Acropolis in Greek means "high city."

Aisle In a church, the space on either side of the nave, set off by rows of pillars.

Amphitheater A circular or oval building with tiered seating and an open central arena, as used by the ancient Romans.

Apse The semicircular or multi-angular space at the end of a church, usually behind the main altar.

Arabesque A complex and elaborate design made up of geometric shapes, flowing lines and intertwining flowers and leaves.

Arcade A series of arches supported by columns, either free-standing or attached to a wall, often forming a covered walkway.

Baldachin A canopy supported by columns, usually placed over an altar, throne or tomb.

Baroque A style of art and architecture characterized by elaborate ornamentation and curved lines that developed during the late Renaissance period. The word *baroque* comes from the Portuguese word for "irregular."

Bay One of the compartments into which the nave of a church is divided; the space between one column and the next.

Bishop A high-ranking clergyman in the Christian Church who has authority over other clergymen and

usually supervises a church district, or diocese.

Buttress A masonry support built up against a wall to resist the outward thrust of an arch or a vault.

Calligraphy Beautiful handwriting.

Cathedral A large church in a city where a bishop has his throne.

Cenotaph A monument or empty tomb honoring a dead person who is buried elsewhere.

Choir The west end of a church where services are sung, usually separated by a screen.

Circus In Roman architecture a long enclosure with round ends,

tiered seating and a central open space.

Clerestory The upper level of a church with a series of windows rising above an adjacent roof.

Cloister An arcade around an open space, usually part of a monastery.

Colonnade A row of columns supporting an entablature or arches.

Concrete Cement mixed with coarse and fine aggregate such as pebbles, sand, crushed stone or bricks.

Cornice The projecting upper part of a wall or entablature.

Crypt A space under a building set aside for burial purposes.

Dome A spherical roof, placed like an inverted cup, over a square, circular or multi-angled structure.

Dynasty A succession of rulers belonging to the same family.

Entablature The horizontal upper part of a wall supported by columns and containing the architrave, frieze and cornice.

Façade The exterior of a building on one of its main sides, usually containing an entrance.

Flying buttress An arch that starts from a freestanding pier and presses against a wall to take the thrust of a vault.

Frieze The middle section of an entablature; also the continuous band of relief around the top of a room or building.

Gargoyle A water spout carved as a grotesque figure and used to direct rain away from the roof.

Gothic The name given to the style of architecture prevalent throughout western Europe from the thirteenth to the fifteenth century. It was characterized by pointed arches, ribbed vaulting and flying buttresses.

Islamic Of the Muslim religion, which was founded in the seventh century A.D. by the prophet Muhammad.

Lintel The horizontal timber or stone that spans an opening such as a door or window.

Machicolation A projecting parapet on a castle wall or tower with holes in the floor through which stones or missiles could be thrown onto attackers below.

Mason A person who builds with stone, concrete or bricks.

Mausoleum A magnificent tomb. Originally referred to the tomb of Mausolus, king of Caria in Asia, built in the fourth century B.C.

Medieval Of the Middle Ages, the period between A.D. 1000 and 1400.

Metope Square stone panel between triglyphs in a frieze. Metopes were fixed alternately with triglyphs.

Moghul A member of the Muslim dynasty, founded by Babur, that ruled India from 1526 to 1857.

Mongol A native of Mongolia in eastern Asia. The Mongol conquerors of India were known as Moghuls.

Mortar A mixture of sand, lime and water used to bind blocks of building stone together.

Muslim A believer in Islam.

Nave The main part of a church, stretching westward from the choir.

Obelisk A four-sided tapering pillar topped by a pyramid.

Patron A person, usually wealthy, who supports another person or an activity such as art.

Pediment The triangular panel formed by the sloping eaves and horizontal cornice on the gable of a classical building, later found above porticos, doors and windows.

Piazza An open public square.

Pilaster A rectangular column attached to a wall.

Pilgrim A person who travels to visit a holy place such as a shrine.

Pope The head of the Roman Catholic Church.

Renaissance The term, which literally means "new birth," that was applied to the rebirth of the ancient Roman and Greek style of art and architecture in western Europe during the fifteenth and sixteenth centuries.

Rendering Cement or plaster applied to an outside wall.

Rib In a vaulted ceiling the rib is a structural member that transfers load from the ceiling toward a supporting column.

Ribbed vaulting Delicate stonework that was used to decorate the underside of a roof vault.

Romanesque The name given to a style of architecture developed from Roman architecture and characterized by round arches, heavy pillars, thick walls and small windows. It was popular in western Europe from the ninth to the twelfth century.

Rose window A large, circular window filled with colored glass.

Shrine A holy place that was associated with a saint or a miracle.

Spire The tapering, pointed structure built on top of a church.

Transept The part of a church that projects at right angles to the main building, usually at the point where the nave and choir join.

Triglyph Panel placed between two metopes.

Vault An arched ceiling in stone, brick or concrete.

INDEX